## About the Author

David Amerland is a British journalist born in 1964. He cut his teeth in the ELan pages of *The European* and joined the tide of misfits trawling the writing waves of the world when Bob Maxwell's publishing empire crumbled towards the end of the last century. He has, since, been involved in writing, publishing and web development launching a series of companies which have explored each frontier. He gained valuable experience in running corporations by being actively involved with the John Lewis Partnership between 1995 – 2002. He has used that to help guide corporations which range from leading Printing Companies in Greece to international Food Importers. He knows that all this makes him difficult to categorize while keeping him gainfully employed. He has an abiding passion for martial arts, Zen and surfing and looks for the unity of all things in everything he does. If you happen to find it before him be kind enough to let him know.

He is the author of three previous books: *SEO Help: 20 Steps to get your website to Google's #1 page*, *Online Marketing Help: How to promote your online business using Twitter, Facebook, MySpace and other social networks* and *Brilliant SEO: What you need to know and how to do it*. All have been best-sellers on Amazon across three continents.

GW00481908

# The Social Media Mind

How social media is changing business, politics and
science and helps create a new world order

# David Amerland

**ISBN: 978-1-84481-984-3**

The right of David Amerland to be identified as copyright holder of this work has been asserted in accordance with the Copyright, Designs and Patents Act, 1988. This paperback edition published 2012.

The Social Media Mind: How social media is changing business, politics and science and helps create a new world order

Published by New Line Publishing, a Cool Publications Imprint.

For Neila, no thanks can ever be enough.

David Amerland

# Table of Contents

1

# Social Glue

Early on, at the beginning of this century, I was killing time when I discovered happiness. The Miami James L. Knight Center is the last place where you'd go to feel happy. A busy, glitzy conference centre situated at the heart of Miami's Business District, it thrums with purpose and is usually filled with the kind of people who 'make things happen'. The conference hall I was heading for was small by US standards, a meeting room, providing a more intimate setting for a lecture and the speaker, as I entered and took a place near the back of the room, was busy talking about building bridges and establishing working relationships.

A student of Harvard Psychology department associate, Tal Ben-Shahar, the presenter was talking about happiness and networking. I was in Miami on business, setting up the background for an international martials arts convention which was being held there. With sports organisations travelling in from countries as diverse as Argentina and Australia and the scars of 9/11 still fresh, arranging a convention like this in 2002 involved a lot of paperwork, phone calls, emails and long bouts of waiting for someone to examine and approve submitted travel arrangements and issue visas.

With time on my hands I had rolled up at the Knight Center looking for the lecture on Networking and Happiness, a social psychology approach.

From the beginning I sensed that this was a little different. There were the usual buzzwords of joy, forgiveness, optimism, flow, courage and energy being repeated but it was the reaction of those attending which was different. I was, at the time, working as a PR freelance, used to working under pressure with people who were hungry for success, and the reactions of those attending the lecture were about as foreign to my experience as if they had just landed on Earth from another planet.

Used to sharp, academic questions designed to make those asking them appear clever and make the presenter squirm I was stunned by the sense that these strangers sitting in the room around me shared a genuine curiosity about the import of the lecture which bound them with the presenter and each other in a way I was finding difficult to fathom.

"We're trying to build on the knowledge here," one of the participants at the table I was at eventually offered. He was smiling as he explained this to me, his eyes showing an understanding at my bewilderment which in itself was hard to explain. Ben-Shahar, I found out much later is a psychologist and author who has never pursued a tenure-track position nor published research in professional journals yet his Harvard course on the subject of Positive Psychology received, each time it was offered, such a large enrolment of students that it managed to capture the public's attention.

Positive Psychology, as a field, is barely fifteen years old. For much of its history, psychology has seemed obsessed with human failings and pathology. The very idea of psychotherapy, first formalized by Freud, rests on a view of human beings as broken creatures in need of repair. Freud himself was so profoundly pessimistic about human nature that he often expressed his views that many of our drives are barely in control. The behaviourists who came after him developed a model of human life that has treated us as passive vessels, beings mercilessly shaped by the stimuli and the contingent rewards and punishments that surround us, unable to really help ourselves, let alone determine our own fate.

The horrors of World War II gave rise to psychological research which tried to explain how ordinary people could take part, so calmly, in atrocities which stretched the very limits of what the human mind can endure. Social psychologists, in labs, then carried out experiments which proved that human beings are impressionable, capable of becoming coldly insensitive to suffering when obeying "legitimate" orders or cruelly sadistic when playing the role of prison guard. Research focused on subjects like conformity, neurosis, and depression, because it was felt they revealed the most about how our world worked and how society functioned.

Positive Psychology started in 1998 and its emphasis is not on flaws and perceived weaknesses but on strengths. Its proponents, like Tal Ben-Shahar, look at religion or alcoholism not as a crutch and an addiction, but as evidence of mechanisms which need to be studied more closely. There is much to be learned, for instance, about how the regular practice of meditation or prayer, enhances mental and physical health and how having a support network like Alcoholics Anonymous increases mental strength and helps the individual make much healthier, more positive life choices.

Sitting in that meeting room, that day, I was struck by the fact that for the first time since I had come to Miami, six months earlier, essentially an outsider, charged with a specific task and given an apartment on Miami's prestigious Coconut Grove area and a Porsche Boxster to get around, I felt at total ease. There was no pressure to assert myself or impress anyone. There, amongst a group of complete strangers, I felt, suddenly, that I belonged. I remember leaving the lecture actually smiling.

The feeling stayed with me for days and the impression Social Psychology made on me that day turned me into a believer. As a result I kept close track of developments even after my stint was over and, when back in the UK, the luxury of time I had enjoyed in Miami was a distant, pleasant, memory.

When Princeton University' Nobel-award winning psychologist and behavioural economist, Daniel Kahneman, published a study on social interactions which make us happy I was amongst the first to find it.

Kahneman is an anomaly. A behavioural psychologist who has pioneered work on the psychology of judgement and decision making, he received the 2002 Nobel prize for economics for his work on prospect theory which describes how people make decisions amongst alternatives which involve some risk. By taking economics away from our perception of it as a cut-and-dried science governed by mechanistic principles and placing it within the field of behavioural sciences, Kahneman changed it forever.

In his latest study Kahneman asked thousands of subjects to keep diaries of activities or events feelings, companions, and places, during a day and then identified some correlates of happiness.

Some of the things he found this way were obvious. For example the daily commute to work is a major source of aggravation for many people. Sleeplessness contributes to irritability. Having sex is a major source of feeling good. But there were also some surprises. Spending time with one's kids, for instance, produced more negative feelings than positive ones. A simple gift of flowers could change one's mood both at home and at work for days and socialising came a close second to having sex as a source of positive emotions, which only shows how powerful a force within us is "the need to belong."

The findings of social psychology show that, unexpectedly, our brains are hardwired for spiritual experience and no spiritual experience can even come close to experiencing a sense of joy. A picture of beauty, a scene of incredible serenity, a music score, a deep sense of love, can all bring us to our knees with an overwhelming sense of awe. In terms of developmental stages the capacity to smile in children emerges at the same time as puppies learn to wag their tails and kittens learn to purr. The smile, the wagging of the tail and the purr are all social responses signifying the sharing of joy and they emerge only when our primitive, limbic brains become wired to our more advanced, social forebrains, turning us (along with puppies and kittens) from self-serving, inward looking, singletons to social animals.

The need to be social is fraught with paradoxes. Any form of meditation, in any religion, shows that being aware of the moment brings about a state of mindfulness which is truly engaging and which makes us feel so totally involved in our surroundings and aware as to experience, frequently, well-documented states of euphoria. Mindfulness is enlivening. It produces passionate chains of thought and a true immersion in the world. Yet, paradoxically, the awareness that one is not 'in the moment' requires them to be there, in that moment, in order to notice it.

This is why we are, in general, quite content to go along, being socially apart. Hiding our anxiety, pretending everything is OK, even when it's not, without realising that we are missing out on a crucial part of our lives. Our feelings of depression and isolation then, become the norm. We accept that we are 'small', insignificant, incapable of changing anything in our world and, here's where it gets interesting, not only do we accept this as normal, we accept is as 'the norm.'

There are three things holding us back and keeping us trapped and social psychology details each one: our fear of evaluation, our acceptance of absolutes, and our false ideas about mistakes. All three have the same root cause: our notion that in every situation there is a single hierarchical structure which leads to a single solution. A hot or cold. A right or wrong. A black or white, proposition. This also guides our view of the world and our sense of our place in it. Yet the world is a social construct. Mistakes are not mistakes in all contexts. Absolutes do not exist and there is more than one way to arrive at any one state in it. To truly understand this, to get into the moment, we need to be capable of noticing things, to be able to see perspective and context and actually discuss it and internalize it.

Einstein put much stock in nurturing the child-like questioning spirit in us which is constantly asking

'Why?'. On the last page of the *Whole Earth Catalog* there is a Steve Jobs quote which says: "Stay Hungry. Stay Foolish." Picasso said: "Youth has no age." They were all talking about the same thing. They were talking about the ability to look at the world and experience a sense of excitement and a powerful desire to connect. Essentially a sense of joy at simply being alive. In order to experience the need to share something you have found out and to have the ability to feel that each moment, each experience, is made up of all these different parts, all working together, you need to be aware of where they are, what they are, how they interconnect and how you then connect with them.

This kind of thinking, on a global scale, is a revolution which has the ability to change practically everything.

Social media, in its many guises and many, different functional manifestations, places us on the very cusp, of this revolution. The seemingly simple act of sharing information and communicating with others, provides the social glue we need that keeps us from straying too far from the moment. It keeps us from becoming forgetful and isolated, and unable to experience every moment of life and feel happy doing it. And it is spreading.

Everything is about to change.

David,
Manchester, 2012

# ■Chapter 1
## The Social Media Mind

There is a certain presumption in labelling anything as a 'Mind'. It assumes that something different is going on, something new which has not been met before and which, now, needs to be better understood in order to decide just how it could be utilised in the world of business, science, politics and – even – everyday life.

For better or worse we have taught ourselves that changes in our mindset, in our philosophy and in our point of view need to have a practical angle rather than a theoretical one. We do not condone anything which might hark back to the Romantic Movement lest it taint the technocratic approach which informs much of what makes our western civilization, tick. This is an observation more than a complaint and, in most cases, the approach serves us well.

It serves us so well as a matter of fact that many times we launch businesses based upon our belief about consumer behaviour which is not backed by the hard data we would like to have in order to justify the launch.

It probably says a lot about our world that we crash and burn relatively few times. The majority of the times our woolly beliefs are eventually upheld by hard data which vindicates our initial show of faith.

I mention all this because social media has been no exception. The 'sexy' name, the snazzy label (i.e. social media marketer), the sense that somehow, we get to now speak to the world, all add up to a sense of glamour we find hard to resist and which seems designed to seduce even the staunchest supporter of the scientific method.

With search and optimisation metrics, the different ways by which you measure the effectiveness of what you do, are a crucial element of the job. Social media marketing however has, as you will find out, been plagued by a consistent complaint from both sides of the divide. Marketers complain about long lead times and difficulties in tracking results and clients complain about the inability of marketers to show them hard data verifying the results they are being paid for.

Whilst complaining, both camps engage in social media marketing for much of the same reason. Marketers because they have to pay the bills and clients because they have to make sales to… pay the bills. No one is seriously questioning if social media marketing is working and no one is asking the obvious qualitative question: what exactly is social media marketing?

It is only by asking basic questions that we establish the fundamental analysis upon which something as defining as a true paradigm shift can be based on.

The truth is that social media marketing is not as new as we would like to think, as a matter of fact it's as old as the hills. We have always valued personal opinion and recommendation, our ancestors probably exchanged tips on the best type of rock club to make and the best person, or place, to get the materials from. Our evolutionary hardwiring makes us social by default (a phrase we will come upon again soon in a slightly different context) and our willingness to be social, our desire to be accepted by our peers frequently pushes us into patterns of behaviour which make us prone to the type of mistakes marketers (and politicians) love us to make.

In its purest form social marketing (and I have omitted the word 'media' here by design) is nothing more than the passing of product knowledge and opinion amongst a social group which has a shared system of values and a recognisable identity.

Before writing, advertising and politics were even notions we could consider, much less disciplines we can study and skills we can learn, social marketing was probably the only available means of passing valuable knowledge and experience from one person to another. Our ability to quickly discern the trustworthiness of the source and retain the knowledge must have been an evolutionary benefit because socialisation is an evolutionary trait.

Today we no longer live in caves and no longer need to carry clubs made of stone. We still, however, form social groups with a shared system of values and a recognisable identity and we still count the opinion of those we know and who are part of our social group above what we can find out independently, for ourselves.

## We are natural born storytellers

Telling stories is something all people, everywhere, love to do. My dad used to tell tales of his fishing trips on rubber dinghies which to me, hearing his recounting and having actually been there, bordered on the fictitious.

My friends often talk to me about girls they have seen or incidents they have witnessed in a way which leaves me feeling certain that what I have missed, in each case, is the most beautiful girl on the planet and the most earth-shattering moment of angst, happiness or wonder.

One of my brothers has consistently told me of every girl he has ever gone out with that she is the most beautiful, sexy girl a guy can imagine. We are, it seems, constantly forming a narrative in our heads, there is a running movie going through our minds where we are cast, depending upon the moment and who we are with as either leads or supporting actors.

The plot we run is put together, as we go through the day (and our lives) is edited on the fly, special effects are added, as required, character actors come in and out, rise in importance or drop, until we have a movie we can 'play' at a moment's notice.

The movie, of course, is produced by our memories and our knowledge and, here, you will probably be forgiven for questioning whether we really piece a movie together which is selectively edited, in effect, stretching the truth a little (or a lot) like my dad did with his fishing tales, and perhaps, even, lying to ourselves a little bit.

I could, here, recount the instances in which phrases occur in literature, and even everyday life (such as 'get real' for instance), which remind us that we can deceive ourselves and lie to our own mind but the example would be more effectively illustrated by looking at some scientific research instead.

Neuroscience is a science which aims to uncover the way we use our brain. Those active in it uncover truths which then are used to help us understand just how we function in our own reality. Most science is informed by suppositions which are derived from common sense, which, in turn, become the basis for a working hypothesis.

As happens in most aspects of science, you would expect research to eventually, catch up with the 'gut feeling' which informs the original suppositions. Philosophers, psychologists, and neuroscientists usually consider remembering to be a solitary activity. We envision the lone researcher, lost in contemplation like Rodin's iconic sculpture of the *Thinker*, recalling his past.

In memory experiments, thousands of subjects have sat alone in front of computers or memory drums (older devices designed to present information), or have lain inside giant magnets, duly recollecting events of their lives, while their brains were studied. As a result of all this cumulative work, we have learned much about how remembering works. However, this tradition of research fails to capture a prominent characteristic of everyday remembering which is the social aspect. In everyday life people do not just sit alone and try to remember. They do not engage on their own in thought, reflecting on their past and, perhaps, wondering about their future. People tend to reminisce in groups, whether at family dinners, reunions, or other social groupings.

Memories and the ways we employ them are then important. They not only shape our internal model of what is real but they also become the building blocks of the narratives we tell ourselves and others. They become the storylines running inside our heads which then become externalised and interwoven with those of others and form a much larger, richer tapestry which, eventually, becomes history.

The need to sit around the proverbial fire and storytell is so deep in us, that it has given rise to a multi-billion dollar global industry by the way of films, books and (to a degree) video games. These all explore one aspect of the need to escape and experience a world which is different to the one we live in right now.

Because we are all familiar with make-believe, we are also, most of us, secure in that we, as individuals, would never fabricate the truth, create memories which are not true and then use them as part of our real-life internal narrative. We are confident that the world we see and the world we understand is recorded in our brains as hard-fact neurological equivalents of little 1s and 0s and that we then use these as the building blocks of whatever narrative we star in.

Well, that's what Micah Edelson, Tali Sharot, Raymond Dolan and Yadin Dudai, four neuroscience researchers with the Department of Neurobiology, Weizmann Institute of Science, Israel, expected to find too. To test this they devised a little experiment where they asked groups of volunteers to take part in a simple experiment.

The volunteers were shown a short, documentary style film (to keep it as realistic as possible) where a police arrest was shown. They were then called back three days later and given a questionnaire about it which was devised to test the accuracy of their recollection on the events they had seen on the film. As you would expect, the accuracy levels were pretty high with the participants exhibiting a very good recollection of the events they had witnessed.

The researchers then brought the participants back in, just four days later to answer another questionnaire. This time they wired them up to a brain scanner in order to study the physical changes which occur in the brain and also gave them, under the guise of helping them remember, a memory jogger with purported to show the answers to the questions of the other members of the group. The memory jogger had answers which contradicted the reality of the events the participants had watched on the documentary.

In what must be a worrying result when it comes to sequestered juries debating the fate of an accused, this time nearly 70% of those questioned changed their recollection to conform to what they perceived to be the group norm.

This part of the results of the experiment should not really come as a surprise. We have long known about the peer group pressure issue which makes even the best raised teenager participate in petty vandalism, recreational drug taking, smoking and alcohol drinking in order to fit in with the group norm perception of fun.

We have all been in situations ourselves, as adults, where we have kept our mouths shut or agreed with an opinion we would not normally agree with because we did not want to stick out from the group. Social lying is a verified phenomenon. It is also lying which we engage in knowingly, we do not, for instance, change our opinion about something, we just keep that opinion hidden and appear to have a different public opinion.

The experiment conducted by the researchers in Israel did not place those taking part in it in a situation of peer group pressure, except perhaps in their minds. When almost 70% of them changed their recollection of events they had witnessed in the film, to conform, they did so because some perhaps felt a certain amount of peer group pressure and because, quite possibly, some were unsure of the accuracy of their own recollection.

Conscious lying and even social lying, the so-called, fibbing or white-lying, is hardly new and hardly earth-shaking and unlikely to produce any paradigm shift no matter how widespread it might be as a practice. This is part of what we call public conformity and each of us practices this every day. We might, for instance, privately disagree with possession of marijuana being a criminal offence but publicly we support it because to speak out for it will class us as either pot-heads, or as people who want the law to be "soft on drugs".

The researchers understood this so they took their experiment one step further. A week later, the participants were called back again to undergo yet a third bout of questioning about the events they had witnessed in the film. This time they were also told that the answers they had received help with last time had actually been drawn from random samples rather than the group replies to the questions. The researchers were meticulous, they screened the participants for doubts as to the legitimacy of the previous answers (which would indicate that they would critically re-examine their own recollection and behaviour) and excluded any from the group.

The results, again undertaken with an fMRI brain scanner showed that almost half of those questioned persisted with their false memories of the events they had supposedly witnessed in the film. This meant that despite the fact that now there was no reason for social lying, nevertheless, almost half of those questioned had changed their story and were now sticking to it. Even more interesting is what was recorded by the fMRI equipment.

It is one thing to lie to others. It is less understandable how one can knowingly lie to one's self. White lies, fibbing and even bigger porkies are all part of the social contract. We never say completely what we think because the narrative which runs in our heads, works in advance to bring up all alternative scenarios and consequences and then gives us all the possible options to choose from. So, at work, we agree that our boss' inane marketing plan is "super", we always say "No" to the question "does my bum look big in this?" and we never tell our best friend he's acting like a jerk, when he is.

We also get into the habit of labelling our cowardice and lack of action as "strategic thinking", always tell ourselves that we did OK "under the circumstances" and actually believe that the diet, training plan, secret work project, novel, we have been planning to start is something we will begin "next week".

All of these activities are part of the storytelling we do. The narrative we fashion. Now here's the interesting thing, by mentioning the words 'narrative' and 'storytelling' we assume that there is some kind of master editor inside our heads who takes bits and pieces of what we see, hear and understand, examines them critically under some self-defined spotlight of criteria, knowingly discards what cannot be used and knowingly puts together what can be used in order to end up with 'our story'.

This scenario assumes full consciousness of our decisions in view of a social context, which means that really, deep down, we are fully aware of what is real and what is not, of what is the truth we have witnessed and what is the lie we have just told. We choose to lie because we think it will help us fit in perhaps, or make us sound better, or raise the perceived value of ourselves in the eyes of other members of the group, but though we do so, we believe that when we do lie, we know the difference between lies and the truth. Well, in the fMRI study the results told a different story.

By comparing the physical states of the brain between the two instances: one, when the participants were being guided in their own answers by the false answers of what they thought was the rest of the group and two, when they had to remember, entirely on their own and free from any kind of peer group pressure or the notion that social lying would give them any advantage, the researchers were able to see at work, the reality of the brain itself, which in turn shapes the world we think we see.

When it comes to storing memories there are two centres in the brain which are. The first one is the hippocampus, first discovered by the Venetian anatomist Julius Caesar Aranzi in 1587, who initially likened it to a seahorse, using the Latin: hippocampus. It sits inside the media temporal lobe in the brain, it is a paired structure (like the left and right hemispheres of the temporal lobes) and belongs to the limbic system, one of the oldest, fundamental parts of the brain itself.

The second centre involved in the storage of memories is the amygdala (itself comprised of several regions) which is also part of the limbic brain. Research has shown that the amygdala in the brain is used to perform a primary role in the processing and memory of emotional reactions, one of its primary roles in the formation and storage of memories associated with emotional events. It plays a significant role in the formation and retention of lifelong memories.

By comparing the states of their subjects' brain between the times when they knowingly were lying because of the social pressure introduced which induced them to do so and when they had no real reason to lie, the researchers were able to examine the differences between the two states. What they discovered was that a co-activation between the hippocampus and the amygdala showed that the brain was actively replacing one set of memories with another, essentially changing the physical record of its recollection of the events the participants in the study had witnessed and, thereby, substituting real memories with false ones.

It was like someone had gone into the hard drive of a computer which held a record of a video showing an event and had edited it, changing some of the facts to fit a different narrative storyline. Anyone subsequently viewing the video, without any knowledge of the edit, would have to accept it as truth.

Essentially what the research carried out in Israel showed was that our natural-born storytelling ability, which is part of the armoury of tricks we use to survive in a social group situation, can be co-opted by clever social media manipulation, to make us lie convincingly to ourselves without our own knowledge.

Stunned by their findings the researchers wrote:

*"Altering memory in response to group influence may produce untoward effects. For example, social influence such as false propaganda can deleteriously affect individuals' memory in political campaigns and commercial advertising and impede justice by influencing eyewitness testimony. However, memory conformity may also serve an adaptive purpose, because social learning is often more efficient and accurate than individual learning. For this reason, humans may be predisposed to trust the judgment of the group, even when it stands in opposition to their own original beliefs."*

So, in other words, we can be betrayed by our own biology to believe in things which are not real, as if they are.

Why?

As the researchers suggested there are evolutionary benefits to be derived from accepting the wisdom of the group, but surely that does not work when it leads to self-delusion.

The answer lies elsewhere. And it has to do with speed, or rather the speed of change we experience in our lifetime.

# The world changes faster than we do

Whether we like it or not, we are locked into a two tier universe. In the first tier is biology and biological processes (and this governs neurophysiology) and in the second tier there is technology which is the main engine powering the core changes in our civilization.

Biology works slowly, changes happening in this field take decades to make themselves felt and then decades more to become completely integrated in who we are. Technology works, like the internet, in dog years. Each year of our lives we experience seven years' worth of accumulated technological change.

It is not change itself however which causes problems. It is rather the rate of change and the acceleration we achieve each time we change.

When communication between social groups was limited by the range of a horse, the visibility of a column of smoke signals, how far a human being could walk or how fast a pigeon could fly, social group strategies were different. They would take longer to form and their thrust (so to speak) would also be different, slower, deeper, perhaps more obvious.

The steam engine locomotive and the telegraph changed all that. Suddenly societies and social groups which were far apart appeared to be closer together. Given ample time, for instance, the participants in the Israel study could have, quite possibly, worked out what was real and what was not, deliberated what would really have been of social value to them and what wasn't and they may not have been affected by the planted false responses which then led them to unconsciously falsify the real memories stored in their brains.

Time however is something we have less and less of. Speed changes everything. It changes the required response time to an event, it alters the time available for deliberation and it makes greater and greater demands upon our ability to react properly. What's more, the speed with which everything around us is happening affects us, just like the subjects in the Israel study, in ways which we do not realise.

Take search engines for example. Google has, arguably, been instrumental in bringing order to the often chaotic, information structure of the web.

Search engine optimisers have known all along that human behaviour is in adaptive mode when it comes to search and the web. Anecdotal examples show that many of us rely on Google's ability to auto-correct words and suggest the correct spelling and, therefore use the search engine not only to find items we are not 100% sure how they are spelled, but also to often correct our own bad spelling which probably leads to a weakening of our own spelling skills.

When Google Instant was implemented, for example, it was a piece of programming designed to suggest possible search queries based on anonymously accrued search results in a drop down field right from Google's search box. The intention, from Google, was to help shave seconds off the typing of search queries. The search algorithm did not change and the way websites were being indexed did not change. Yet, this relatively simple change, presented SEOs with a major challenge.

Websites which were either not popular enough or not optimised enough in relation to specific search terms saw their traffic dip sharply as the traditional search pattern of Google users who "rarely get past Page three of the search results" changed to Google users who now simply click on what Google Instant suggests.

As web users we are constantly locked into adaptive learning behaviour. The web is changing at an enormously fast pace and functionality and design develop in a complex feedback cycle where we take the technology developers create (and websites use) and through its use create a demand for the next wave of developments.

Adaptive learning not only makes us enthusiastic early adopters of everything the web has to offer but it allows us to seek innovative ways to use it which will offer us some kind of gain. Sometimes the gain is material as in money, commerce, or even information, and at other times it's a gain in efficiency, like the time saving implementation of Google Instant. Either way adaptive learning behaviour is always 'On' when we work online and it often guides many of our decisions.

Transactive memory is a mind-trick that's always been on, no matter where we are in terms of evolution. Basically, the brain remembers where to get the information it needs (and how) rather than bothering to remember all the information in detail, a little like a summary of something bigger, lying somewhere and waiting for us to access.

In pre-historic societies there were probably 'elders' we would go to when we needed to find out something specific about a hunting area or a type of game. In the more modern world we created 'experts' as a category to source data from with a higher trust factor. Google's ability to search the web and the web's capacity for storing information is the latest evolutionary step in this cycle.

The study called *Google Effects on Memory: Cognitive Consequences of Having Information at Our Fingertips,* was carried out by J. Liu and D.M. Wegner, and it revealed that when it comes to employing transactive memory we have come to rely on the web and search as a means of finding out what we want without having to remember it.

As a potential weakness this is important. It means that the moment our computers are unplugged our wealth of knowledge which we have come to automatically rely upon in our decision making is suddenly much poorer. For me, I know that even recalling when I last baked a birthday cake for my partner, is suddenly a herculean task without my access to Google Calendar (I actually feel a lot more stupid without access to the web).

There is a flip side to this however which is brighter. By avoiding filling our heads with clutter we free our capacity to analyse data and can suddenly focus on the big picture. Suddenly we become strategists, able to plan in a bigger scale, think in a wider view and dip into detailed information selectively, as the need arises, in order to better evaluate our decision making.

In short, by using technology as an adjunct to memory we short-circuit biology (and evolution) and things begin to get really interesting.

It is no accident that we live in a time of rapid technological development led by information processing. Incidentally, this makes the use of search on the web and the ability of search engines like Google to unearth the information we need, all the more crucial. It is not even inconceivable that, at some not too distant future, websites will be required to be search compliant (which means optimized) like email marketing has to be spam compliant today.

It is this collision between the technical and the human which creates the crucible out of which so many new possibilities arise and so much excitement is generated. The web, clearly, is not just driving eCommerce and information, it is also shaping the evolution of human intellect and that is something that is at the heart of what having a social media mind and social media mentality really means.

It was Nicholas Carr who poked his head above the parapet first when in a provocatively titled article published in *The Atlantic* magazine asked "Is Google making us stupid?". Of course, the headline of the article notwithstanding, he did not really mean that Google was really making us stupid. He was using Google as the most prominent search engine in the world to point to the fact that technology and the web were changing the way we think by fostering a shorter attention span.

His argument was that the narrow-beamed attention of concentration which we used to be able to bring to bear upon text, when reading in old-fashioned paper, is no longer available to us, as we are assailed from all sides by information which is crying for our attention and we become, as a result, experts at skimming over articles, absorbing details on the fly and moving on.

27

Carr's argument in the article and in a book which subsequently came out titled *The Shallows: What the Internet Is Doing to Our Brains* is as far-reaching as it is wide-ranging, covering the introduction of time and motion studies and scientific management and the impact the widespread use of the typewriter had on the style of writing authors like Nietzsche and his contemporaries. Its premise however is simple enough: by being forced to work at a speed outside our normal range, our thought processes may be 'flattening' using their unexpected twists and turns which lead to insights and associations and sudden discoveries and we may all be becoming more machine-like in our approach, AIs of a sort.

Carr's arguments have sparked off a lively debate amongst neuroscientists and sociologists, some of whom dismiss his thoughts out of hand and others who entertain their value and the plausibility that he might be right.

Bearing in mind that even Plato, rued the use of writing and considered it an instrument which would destroy mnemonics forever (it turns out he was right), we have to consider that technology has always affected us. The development of a social media mind is just that, adopting a mindset which understands the medium and its nuances, feels at home within it and best allows us to take advantage of what it has to offer.

## The social media mindset

Like any medium of communication social media has its own tropes which must be mastered in order to use it properly.

Just like Shakespeare's prose was unsuitable for the age of the telegraph, for instance, so does the usual way of communicating from a business perspective with its over-worked, corporate-speak appear to be inadequate and counterproductive in the social media age.

You'd think it's easy to change syntax a little and shorten sentences somewhat. It's not. A change in the way we communicate from a syntactical point of view also requires a far more profound and radical change from a thinking point of view.

Whether the change which takes place in our evidently 'plastic' brains makes us less clever (in the traditional view of intelligence) or simply different, and more adaptable and forces us to take steps which allow us to use our brains differently, the certain thing is that social media is changing us.

We are, now, living through a process of transition which will usher us into a new age of communication the likes of which we have never seen before. One which is having an impact across every activity we undertake.

# ■Chapter 2

## Social is the Default Setting

The Facebook f8 conference in September 2011 was different to every other f8 conference before it. Just over two months previously Google had launched its social networking service, Google Plus, and the online tectonic plates had shifted noticeably. For the very first time since its inception Facebook was on the receiving end and scrambling to catch up and all from a player it had all but discounted in the social networking stakes.

There is an unwritten rule in business which is echoed in the boxing ring: if you are getting hurt, don't show it. At the f8 in September Facebook was carrying out business as usual. The presentation, jokes and the staple appearance of its founder, Mark Zuckerberg, were all there. But just like a boxer who's been caught by some heavy blows hides the damage through more movement and a brave show of energy, so was Facebook's presentation a little more energetic, trying to dazzle with style rather than substance, presenting things to come like they were already there and explaining a new vision which represented a change in direction in an attempt to wow the participants.

Stung by Google+ or not, at the f8 conference Zuckerberg made a number of significant announcements regarding Facebook and its re-design. He explained the importance of Timeline, its new user interface, and the expanded ability of both Facebook Connect (which allows you to log onto a website without registering, just by using your Facebook login and password) and the Facebook 'Like' Button and he summed it all up beautifully by saying that Facebook was no longer focused on growth. It was, instead, focused on increasing the depth of its socialising influence through the totality of its members' online activity. "Social is going to be the default on the web," he said.

The implications of this new vision are big and divisive. The truth is however that while Zuckerberg was applying this to the new functionalities of Facebook and presenting it as something entirely new, he was thinking as a programmer rather than an end-user. The fact is that social has always been the default mode on the web.

## But we are all connected!

There is a thing about the web which we often forget. Developers, journalists, marketers and designers (and pretty much anyone associated with anything which has to do with the online world) have, at some time, all forgotten the basic rule which drives the online world and makes everything else possible: the internet is people.

The reason we forget is simple. The moment we have within our grasp the capability to implement some new functionality, programming, design or type of marketing, the logistics required to make it happen are usually so complicated that it is easy to lose sight of the wood for the trees.

We all want to connect and be social. But we cannot all be social butterflies or networking lions. People interaction is frightening, rife with opportunities for rejection, disappointment and disenchantment. The web, like a magic wand, does away with all this. It allows us to be social whenever we choose, however we choose, entirely on our terms, dealing from within the centre of our comfort zone and terminate the contact safely and without hurting anyone's feelings.

From the safe isolation of our bedrooms, living rooms and home offices, we become, suddenly, ethereal presences cruising along the eternal night of cyberspace, hooking up, making friends, solving problems, averting crises, playing games, sharing experiences and doing everything we would do in an ordinary social setting if we only could be made to feel that we are better looking, more successful, more intelligent and more witty than we really are.

It seems perverse that we can be more social than anyone would have thought possible when we are at our most anti-social, locked away from the world and silently staring at a computer screen, but that, as psychologists will tell you is the way we operate. When we are at the maximum of our disconnect we also are ready to connect and feel the need for interaction.

The history of the web and its development, as a matter of fact, reads like a shopping list for the 'lonely man's connective tools to the world'. Email, forums, chat rooms, ICQ, IRC, instant messengers, commenting systems, online voting systems, social networks, Twitter. Each of these has been another step towards greater and greater interactivity, connection, interaction and engagement. Their success has been made possible not because we want someone to market to us, or because we feel the need to get our social profile 'out there', but because we cannot sit and stare at a computer screen without feeling the need to connect with someone else, even if it's for five minutes.

As I am writing these words I have taken no fewer than four breaks to check my Facebook and Google Plus accounts, to see what's new, who interacted with posts I commented on, who 'Liked' or 'Plus Oned' what I posted and who sent me private messages. I am not unusual.

Journalist friends tell me that making deadlines these days, a thing which should be easier because a lot of the legwork of research is done online, from home, is actually more difficult than when we were all stuck in newsrooms somewhere, because they cannot switch off from checking emails, messages and their social profiles.

We are all at it, it seems and there is no stop in sight. The social web is expanding both in reach and depth. It is making it easier to bridge online and offline activities through ultra-portable tablets and smartphones. It is expanding its reach to cover eCommerce as well as leisure activities and it is making it easier for us all to connect and interact, share ideas and insights, give advice and find solutions to our problems.

Why?

Because in the chatter we create we each feel empowered within our world, on our terms and within the limits and limitations of our choosing. We can have 'bad' days where we spend 16-hours online chatting with friends or simply eavesdropping on the misfortunes of others. We can become disembodied angels capable of peering almost everywhere. Facebook teens line up to show us their bedrooms and pictures of themselves taken in their underwear. We see places so far away and so culturally different from our own experiences that they may as well be on the dark side of the moon. We see relationships breaking up and new ones starting.

We find people we like and we try to befriend them. We use the net to be unfaithful, to find shortcuts to our work or homework, to do research, to spy on friends or competitors, to become voyeurs, to find out information, to do, in short everything we do as human beings only more privately and with greater efficiency than ever before.

Social, for us, has always been a default function and it has had nothing to with functionality. As a matter of fact when it comes to what is possible, the web is always playing catch-up to our needs.

## The dark side of the net

There is a dark side to all this of course. Tomes have been written about the 'dangers' of the web. I am writing here 'dangers' because we are all adults and capable of dealing with risks and dangers almost anywhere.

Depending on who you are willing to listen to about it, the web can also be a dark, lonely place where all sorts of perversions can occur. Nigerians can offer you millions if you only just manage to part with your account details, loose women will corrupt your soul, dating networks for married people will lead you down a path which only the ungodly ever dare to tread and the ability to buy almost anything from the privacy of your own home will have you ordering the kind of music that's fit only for Satanic rituals after midnight.

The fact that almost everyone has an opinion about how 'bad' the web can be and is willing to share it only testifies to the power it exerts upon us, as individuals.

Of course there is a dark side to the web. I dreamt about it once (and it's not the kind of dream you think).

I had this dream in which my every move was somehow recorded and my every action observed. I felt that there was an unseen sky above me where an invisible, unblinking eye watched and recorded everything I did. The porn sites I visited (or didn't), the lethal weapons page I checked out, the revolutionary group I befriended on Facebook and the poisons website I spent an hour reading, at – it all got recorded.

In my dream I was walking in circles, beginning to panic, feeling suffocated and yet seeing no one. The circles got smaller and smaller and my sense of panic was heightened, until I felt that there was nowhere for me to hide. I curled up then, in the foetal position, a tiny dot in an endless plain under a sky that missed nothing.

That dream, potentially, can come alive.

The funny thing is that what can make it possible is exactly the same 'social' trend which has made the web what it is, today.

## It's all about the data

We live in a world like that of the Matrix. Hiding behind the code are agents, snoopers, cookies and spyware, all designed to track down who we are, what we do, where we go and what we like.

In the web of the future there really will be no place to hide. Why? Funnily enough because, paradoxically, this also helps us experience it better.

Everything you put online, from the status updates to your Facebook account to the content you share, the content you create and the web pages you visit, has value. In the duality which is the web, the value can, depending upon who you choose to listen to, be good (i.e. it will help you do things better, faster and with greater benefits to yourself) or bad (the stark landscape of my dream).

For all its vast size the web is tiny. It represents just a small portion (probably equivalent to no more than 10%) of all the things we do offline. eCommerce, for instance, which is worth, globally many hundreds of billions of dollars, represents no more than 8% of all retail transactions.

In the offline world with its inherent messiness and 'noise' everything becomes small, fragmented, hit and miss. Compare it, if you like to an open-air fish market where with the produce sitting on a ticking clock, each fisherman who has a stall is busy trying to yell louder than everybody else in a bid to attract your attention.

In that noisy marketplace it is difficult to tell with any kind of precision just what it is that motivates you to buy. Is it the size of the fish? The look in their eyes? The way they have been packed? The fact that the fisherman who sold it to you was the only one who was clean shaven?

Really what motivated you in that setting is anybody's guess. Now compare that to the fish market equivalent online. You click and go to each digital stall. You read about the history of each type of fish and what they are known for (some are tastier than others, some are better grilled and some can only be boiled). You check out the fisherman's humane way of fishing and the fact that he is fully compliant with international fishing laws regarding the size of his catch. You find out that he contributes to the 'Save the Whales' fund and Greenpeace. Finally you check out the reviews left by previous buyers and then you decide whether you will buy or not.

All of the things you check out are recorded. If your digital fisherman is truly web-savvy he will know whether before you decided to purchase you looked at the fact that he contributes to Greenpeace or reviews left by other shoppers and he will adjust his digital fishing stall to more prominently display one or the other of these things. He will then track to see if the changes increase conversions from online visitors to fish buyers.

If he gets this right, and provided he does not lie, this will benefit you. You will be able to make a purchasing decision easier, faster, based upon what is ultimately important to you as a buyer.

But suppose out fisherman wants to sell things very badly and is not so scrupulous. He knows you were on his digital fishing stall. He knows what you looked at and where you went and, should he decide to track you after you have left his stall without making a purchase, he will also know that you bought some fish from his competitor and then you went to a dating website. Before you know it, you are receiving anonymous messages warning you that your dating history is about to become public knowledge and only the regular purchase of some fish from a well-known digital fish stall is likely to keep it a secret.

Farfetched? Maybe. Yet my crude example, rough as it may be, exactly illustrates the issues associated with the real dark side of the web.

Data, online is currency. Advertisers, companies and even ordinary one-man outfits would love to get their hands on it, or at the very least, have the ability to target you because they know your preferences. When it comes to data there are two companies which are masters at collecting it and then using it to give you what they think will help make your online life easier and, perhaps, better. The first one is Google, whose dominance in search has given it the ability to collect massive amounts of data. The second one is Facebook whose global size to almost 10% of the world's population has placed it in an ideal position to collect extremely detailed data about your preferences, likes and dislikes, curated, mostly, by you. Funnily enough neither company has enough data, yet.

Google, until now, has been missing out the ability to refine its data through socialised components. It may, for instance, know that when you go online you start the day by search 'News in Scarborough' but it does not know whether you are male or female, your occupation, age group and friends.

Facebook is the other way around. It knows all there is to know about you which you have placed in the Facebook environment, but the moment you leave that it knows next to nothing about you and what you do.

Faced with a similar problem – how to acquire more data about you and refine it both Google and Facebook have opted to respond in a similar way: they have each decided to try and each be a bit more like the other.

Google has tackled social through the launch of its Google Plus social network. Facebook, with the announcement of its Timeline at the f8 Facebook conference and the increased capability of the functionality of its 'Like' button and Facebook Connect, is trying to become as good as Google at collecting web-surfer data.

There is an aspect to this which is critical and which we need to examine in a moment, but right now, what is important is that by acquiring this data each of these two massive organisations will feed a trend which has been evidenced on the web for some time and which is split into three separate but related streams: Personalisation, Localisation and Socialisation.

Taken to an extreme extrapolation this means that, for example, Google's search engine would know exactly where you were, and know what you are looking for, the moment you brought the page up and would be preparing to give you all the results of Pizza restaurants within a 10 mile radius, complete with reviews, addresses and phone numbers, before you had even finished typing in the second 'z' in the search engine query box.

It was Larry Page, one of Google's founders, who famously said that "the perfect search engine would know what you want before you did." That search engine does not exist, yet, but the road to it is paved with data.

So, what's the problem? Well, it has to do with Orwell and personal freedom and it also has to do with the free flow of information, or at least, our ability to discover it, and its cost.

One of the most frequently misquoted sayings is Stewart Brand's "Information wants to be free." It is misquoted because it is nearly always taken out of context.

Brand founded the *Whole Earth Catalog*, an infrequent publication which served as type of manifesto of ideas and hipness for an entire generation. In 1984 he was discussing his philosophy with Apple co-founder Steve Wozniak and in the context of that conversation gave us the first, recorded instance of his saying: "On the one hand information wants to be expensive, because it's so valuable. The right information in the right place just changes your life. On the other hand, information wants to be free, because the cost of getting it out is getting lower and lower all the time. So you have these two fighting against each other."

Brand was right. The tension between these two drives gives us the dual nature of the web we experience today.

# ■Chapter 3
## Angels and Demons in Cyberspace

Is the web good or bad? How would you know? How could you know? The very notion of something as massive and pervasive as the web being 'good' or 'bad' smacks of oversimplification and the kind of kindergarten mentality which I detest. Yet, take a very narrow point of view on anything and it can easily be attributed notional qualities which are more suited to individuals than tools and the web is a tool.

It is, however, the kind of tool which can literally change your life. I use the word 'tool' here of course in a functionality sort of way. The web is there to help us do things – but in reality it is an enabling environment in which we place 'tools' in the form of websites, applications, messaging services, eCommerce platforms and so on, in order to build a hierarchy of sorts which will form a meaningful digital space.

When all this first started out I was working for *The European*, back then on its last legs and in the newsroom we'd discuss two things: the kind of pictures we needed to illustrate the 'Information Super-Highway' (cue for journalists shooting road-signs, trains, buses and automobiles) and the fact that though we all called it the electronic frontier because it was so new and felt relatively untamed, it would not last.

The pictures and articles and documentaries from back then now make me cringe (it *was* last century) but the discussions were spot on.

While we all fret against authority we are ill-suited for living in lawless, disorganized frontiers. Our minds crave some kind of structure, our lives want to have a certain sense of hierarchy and though we do not want to consciously submit to any form of oversight or control, we do want to have things working and for that we are willing to give up some freedom.

The world we live in is a complex one. Beneath its relatively calm surface there are many interactions constantly taking place and the dynamic which keeps it in place is itself both delicate and complicated.

The easiest way to illustrate this is to think of the recent financial crisis in Europe. Greece, a country with a population smaller than Manchester, UK and a Gross National Product which placed it as the 30th economy in the world, was suddenly capable of holding the world to ransom through an over-leveraged borrowing strategy which had gone wrong, because, a possible default would create a domino effect which could burn Europe and destroy the Eurozone.

The failure of a national economy is always an event which should not be overlooked but it should not be globally catastrophic. The incident with Greece illustrated, very visibly, the under-the-surface interconnections which are now part of our everyday reality. Typhoons in one part of the world affect commodity prices in another. Incompetence in one sphere affects our ability to work in many others.

This narrowing of connections is no accident. The quickening we feel in the world around us, a sense that everything happens with the throttle full on, is the default mode of the web.

I have said, here, that it's an environment and we use tools within it. In truth, what we are doing through our use of websites, the creation of blogs, the intricate web of interactions and relationships we forge and the complicated web tools we use to actually do so, is create a world, every bit as nuanced as the one we have a physical presence in but with significant differences and significantly different potential. It is because of this that it is important to understand the dynamics which currently drive it and, as things have it, also divide it.

## Two sides of the same coin

When it comes to using the web to achieve anything I, you and pretty much most people do not really care who does what and why, or for what reason. What we really want is for no one to bother us too much and things to work, fast, reliably and with the minimum of hassle. That's the way the world of work, works, even online (or should I say, *especially* online).

Now, there is another side to the web. I find the web exciting not just because I make money through it but because I, along with many others I have spoken to, sense that here is an opportunity to do things different. In the bricks and mortar world of last century we were used to being told what we could *not* do, rather than what we could. They (and 'they' becomes a very broad term depending on your own particular experiences) would lay down the law because they were bigger, had been doing it longer, supposedly knew better and had deeper pockets.

The web burnt up all these notions, upset the status quo, made established authority figures look ridiculous and created a real sense of excitement that things could change.

When we look at all this through the looking glass of posterity we can see that there has now been a shift of the web being a place where kids with brains, an idea and a thousand dollars in their pocket could make millions to a place where corporate presences with large budgets and teams of people begin to rule, again.

This is true, it has happened, it is happening as we speak, but not because the web has changed from what it was. The shift we notice is not because the 'dream' if we could call it that, of talent and ideas winning over money and manpower, has evaporated. On the contrary the dream is more alive than ever. Examples of Mashable (a one-man technology blog turned into a million dollar empire), the milliondollarhomepage (a 'lazy' student's unwillingness to get a summer job turned into a million dollars) and even Twitter (an online SMS service with no monetization plan), all indicate that the 'dream' is alive and well and fuelling a new generation of start-ups, with its own brand of Young Turks, ready to challenge the entrenched establishment. It is this dream of being this free, of creating something out of nothing (or very little) and then having it make a difference that drives us.

The reason corporations appear to have again become dominant is because the web itself and those who live in it are now getting into the phase where they need to feel a sense of trust in those thy deal with, online.

Even when there is no money transaction involved none of us want to feel that the information we are consuming came from someone's slanted, personal agenda and has little basis in fact.

One thing established businesses have always done well is project that sense of solidity and foster trust.

This does not kill the dream which started it all. We all want to succeed. We all want our ventures to become huge. Money is part of the drive but money is not all (or maybe not even any) of the motivation which drives us, which makes us spend countless hours online which forces us to multi-task through a screen instead of taking long walks outside in the park.

The motivation which keeps our nose to the grindstone is that what we do matters to more than just us. This is what the web has changed. By empowering us, as individuals to 'do' things, to create, organise, promote and develop it has also enabled us to connect on a scale and a level which prior to the web, would have been unthinkable. We call this today the 'social drive' I suspect it will not be too long before we start to call it the 'social imperative' but, deep down, whatever it is that we eventually decide to label it, it simply is the human need to connect. This connection then, more often than not, leads to the next natural step: the need to change the world, to fashion it in a better image than the one we already have. To fix at least some of its ills and create a much fairer arena in which to work and play.

Even when operating within the very narrow confines of an online business, the sense that we can change the world through the creation of money and wealth (which cascades down to others), training, jobs, more people, is still there, just under the surface, like an itch that will simply not go away.

Ask anyone to quantify this and they can't. Get into any conversation involving the web and before too long it surfaces. Why?

To me, this is the social element at work. The web empowers us and with power, most people, want to do some good. They want to leave behind an imprint which has nothing to do with commerce, money and work and a whole lot to do with simply helping others and shaping the world.

These two elements: the drive to do things online, to set up businesses, to create web platforms, to develop websites, to find niches to work in and the more deep-seated but present need to do something which is altruistic, are part of the same coin.

The web has the ability to simplify concepts and create a starkness where none existed before. Divorced of the nuances of body language and visual cues our online interactions are simplified and magnified. It is a dangerous combination. It leads to persistence, obsession and passion and the web has been fuelled, since its beginning by all three.

Like any medium which has the capacity to leech us out of our own shell, the web can, sometimes bring out of us not just the things which are desirable and

46

good, but also the side which is deplorable and bad. This is a constant not just for individuals but also for corporations.

We started this discussion considering that as long as we can get things done it really does not matter what kind of place the web is or who runs it. But because we are more than commercial automatons bent on creating a working presence online we also have to consider how the web is shaping up and the kind of online world we ultimately want to inhabit.

## Facebook vs Google+

There is nothing like a sensationalist headline to draw attention to polarized issues and, perhaps, oversimplify the argument. Until very recently Facebook vs Google+ was just one of them because, in reality, Google+ (Google's own social network) is nothing like Facebook.

Facebook is, and has always been, a "walled garden" with a set of data (its so-called Social Graph) which is closed to users outside it and only transparent to search engines at a layer or two and Google+ is (and has been) a set of socialising tools which can be used to create a level of folksonomy which Google's sensitive but taxonomic search algorithm has so far lacked.

Any suggestions that somehow Google+ would 'kill' Facebook were an expression of wishful thinking from the masses (and there are many) who were dissatisfied with Facebook's immature, autocratic, 'take-it-or-leave-it' approach to handling complaints from users on its network.

The differences between the two still persist and if anything have now been magnified. Before the

September 2011 Facebook f8 conference Facebook's strategic re-positioning with Microsoft and its partnership with Twitter led to a certain level of disgruntlement and charges that somehow 'Facebook was losing its identity'. There were articles in the press which mentioned that it was moving away from being a place where you went to meet all your friends to being a place where business went to market to you more precisely.

As far back as March 2010 I had argued, mainly on my blog, that Facebook, whatever features it implements, has always been a place where your data is not your own and, since it's their website, its management will do whatever they want, any way they want it, no matter what you say. Expecting it to be otherwise seemed, to me, illogical.

The truth is that when it came to being social Facebook has always wanted to control as much of the web as it could. There are good reasons for this and they all have to do with search.

Building a good search engine is incredibly expensive (as Microsoft found out with BING) and incredibly difficult as (Yahoo! discovered with their own failed efforts). Google has got such a good grasp on this that whatever its competitors may do they are likely to still be left behind getting crumbs off a pie which seems to be almost all Google's.

Google search, however, no matter how powerful and sensitive it is, has always battled with SEOs who (by the nature of the job) look for ways to either game or 'help' the search engine rank websites on its search index as high as possible.

Google's Panda update of its search algorithm was introduced in March 2011 and then went through three, separate iterations to refine it in May, June and July 2011 and a number of refinements since. The update was a much-needed sensitisation of search. Its aim was to get rid of spam websites and content farms which dominated the web through high-volume, low-value content and were squeezing out sites from Google's first page which could provide real value to its end users.

In developing its powerful search algorithm Google has used the end-user experience as a yardstick. This has been the drive behind such features as Google Instant and its subsequent refinements, such as webpage preview in the search results page and the loading speed of a website being used as an SEO metric. As a matter of fact every Google refinement in search is intended to maximise the ease and good impressions the end-user has of it.

The basic assumption here is that search is a tool which needs to be fast, relevant and reliable. While Google can do a lot to help with speed and stability, relevancy and reliability in the quality of the search results is harder to guarantee. Indexing on the web is carried out by machines (or coded programs if you will, called bots) and this makes it very difficult to assess something as nefarious as 'quality'.

To get round this issue Google (and almost every other worthwhile search engine out there) use social cues as one of the corroborative metrics to rank a website. Because social cues (which includes things like social bookmarking, online shares of content, Tweeting, Facebook 'Likes' and mentions) are people driven,

Google uses (where it can) your surfing behaviour, and mine, as an adjunct to its search engine to create a simulated contextual semantic search engine where results are curated not just by the power of the search algorithm Google has devised but also by human input.

The reason search is so important is that without it, on the web, you will never find anything. More than that, by finding the right things at the right time, with search you create a commercial dynamic where information has real value and pixels and 1s and 0s can be translated into cold, hard cash for businesses and search engine companies alike.

At the end of the day it is about money. Facebook in 2010 made just shy of $5 billion and Google reported revenues of $9.03 billion for quarter two of 2011 (ending in June 30). The numbers are large enough to illustrate the issue in very stark, but hopefully comprehensible, terms.

Whoever controls the best search has created a money-making machine the like of which few can imagine – Google, as it stands right now is a case in point. When we talk commerce however the pressures are such that it becomes hard to understand the other principles involved. The web is a very exciting place not just because we can get online and use pixels to make money but because we get a sense that size, the depth of your pocket and manpower do not matter as much on the web as they do offline.

A guy working from his garage, with a website, a good grasp of social media marketing and a hot idea has got the opportunity to create an online sensation and beat companies which are bigger in every way. Viewed in this light the web has not become the latest frontier (with the unacknowledged implication that it needs taming), it has become the next step in mankind's technological evolution, allowing us to do more things, faster, better and cost-efficiently than ever before. As such it has spawned a new class of digital workers capable of calling 'home' any place where there is a computer and a good internet connection.

It is this egalitarian space where one could 'stake' their website on that is now under threat.

Google makes no effort to hide the fact that its mission statement is "to index the world's information". At the same time the company motto is "Do no Evil" and, as such, it has become a guiding principle in much of what the company does and how it conducts itself and though it may not always get it pitch-perfect it has yet to act in a way which can be said to have gone against the grain of its motto.

Now the Facebook slogan is "Facebook is a social utility that connects you with the people around you". I won't go here into an exposition on how Facebook states nothing about its intent and everything about its function nor that nowhere in anything Facebook has ever done have we come across any statements which might act as its moral compass, so to speak. To examine each company through the lens of their slogans is self-limiting and extreme. It would discount the fact that both are global corporations with a powerful dynamic guided by the profit principle.

So let's, instead, do the clever thing and look at their fundamentals in search not of differences but of similarities.

Both Google and Facebook, at core, are after the same thing: our data. They want to know everything about you in order to build a better contextual engine.

Now, contextual engines are about a trend on the web which has only accelerated I wrote an article forecasting it at the beginning of 2010, namely, the three vertical fronts of personalisation, localisation and socialisation. Though search is becoming better and better the web and its technologies are always changing in a game which is evolving so fast that search engines, whose creators out of necessity need to use data in order to help them take their evolutionary steps, will always play catch-up.

There is a partial exception to this (only partial) and that is in the creation of the semantic web. This is a relatively simple idea with a complex execution. At its core the idea of the semantic web is that everything which gets put online, from a simple link to a website to a picture and its alt text, have been exhaustively described in a way which makes it easy for a search engine bot to index, assess and categorise.

In a small scale experiment (like say a university) this can happen no problem, mainly because no one has any hidden agenda, or at least if they have it does not impact on search, everyone works off the same page (i.e. they all want to find data fast, efficiently and accurately) and they all, more or less work towards the same thing. Expand this to the vastness of the web with its myriad of complex relationships, agendas, different interests and degrees of capability, knowledge and skill and you begin to realise the magnitude of the problem.

While the task may seem daunting there is a way around it and Facebook showed it, first. Mainly, within

Facebook's closed environment, the data input by its hundreds of millions of users belongs to Facebook which repurposes it in ways it sees fit. So when you and I, for instance, input our hobbies, these immediately fall into a category Facebook can use to better present content to us and which marketers can use to better advertise to us. Because in Facebook's closed, exotic environment, all data belongs to Facebook to do as it pleases with, it has managed, with a vastly inferior search engine, to present advertisers with the option to drill down so far into the demographics of its membership that they could choose to target, if they wanted to, out of Facebook's 800 million members, only 18-22 years old, women, from Pennsylvania who were interested in cycling.

This level of targeting is something Google could only dream of doing.

Now, here's the funny thing. I am on Facebook and I have been a Google user since its inception. Between the two of them Google knows far more about me than Facebook. Yet, when it comes to advertising, Google has a less refined ability to target me precisely than Facebook. The reason for this paradox is that Google actually respects the privacy of my data. Although it mines it just like Facebook, the company goes to great lengths to preserve anonymity and protection while Facebook works hard to get me to share as much as possible. Google randomizes the data to create a data-range which protects the end-users but also makes it difficult for advertisers to target them.

Facebook's success did not go unnoticed by Google. When Facebook closed its social graph to the Google bot, Google created its own social network,

Google+. And here is where the similarities clearly make the differences in approach, stand out. Both Google+ and Facebook are social networks. But while everything I put in the latter is owned by it, all my data, content and work in Google+ belongs to me. Should I decide to close my account I can download my data and do whatever I want with it, Google+ loses the right to use it in any shape or form. More than that, while Facebook is trying to get hold of everything I do in as many ways as possible, Google+ gives me the tools to share as much or as little as I want with anyone I want, whenever I want and to add to this, Google, uses the data it accumulates through all this interaction in a far more anonymous way than Facebook has ever done.

## The web is being divided

The announcements Zuckerberg made at the 2011 Facebook f8 conference regarding Facebook's Open Social Graph are a little disingenuous to say the least. He made a big show, for instance, of the fact that social applications in websites will make it easier for you to share without explicitly agreeing (the so-called "frictionless sharing"). He mentioned the fact that Facebook was bringing out tools to help socialise the web and he made it clear that Facebook's focus now is on websites (which it wants to get data from) and developers (which it needs in order to progress).

The word 'Open' in front of the Social Graph reminds me, a little, of the way the Republic of Congo, arguably one of the most inhospitable places on Earth to anyone with a liberal streak who is not totting a massive weapon and is backed by a personal army, uses the word 'Democratic' in front of its name, like having it there, instantly makes it so.

The deal, as Zuckerberg presented it was that websites will help Facebook mine the data of those who use them and, in return, they will receive exposure to the network(s) of friends those visitors have on Facebook.

The point is that after remaining behind its walls for so long, spurred by the launch of Google Plus, Facebook is now launching an offensive, using the widespread use of its 'Like' button and a new raft of systems to help gather ever more data.

Why Does Any of This Matter?

Well, if you are interested in marketing your business, creating an online brand, or simply surfing the web and having a great time, in the short-term I guess (and probably in the medium term too) the answer is that it does not matter who mines your data.

Whether it's Google or Facebook you will still be able to carry on as usual. The Facebook offensive however with the proposed Timeline and sharing (Zuckerberg calls it 'social') as default, means that the shape of the web to come will be dictated by the winner. Either we will have, for instance, an ecosystem in which the end-user and his experience is the focus and everything else follows (the Google Philosophy) or we will be forced to eat crow, and accept an ecosystem which treats the end-user with contempt because, after all, when you have a huge chunk of the world's population in your membership a single account does not matter (the Facebook approach).

Now, I work online and really love the fact that I can go anywhere and do anything and 'see' anything without anyone bothering me and me bothering anyone. Websites which make me jump through hoops are never visited again, I never give out more information than I absolutely have to and, though much of my career is and has been on the web and working online, I maintain as private a presence as I can. Currently I use Google+ and Facebook for marketing and socialising equally and as far as brand affiliations go I try hard to remain neutral.

Logically, whoever wins this battle will dictate much of what the web will become for me and countless other users. I am not advocating anything here in terms of 'do this' or 'don't do that'. The whole point of this discussion is to lay out, as succinctly as possible, the issues involved and the consequences of each possible outcome. It is a slightly polarized view because each player involved stands at an opposite end of the spectrum.

I must hasten to add it is not as black and white as I paint it. After all Facebook plans are, at the moment, just that – plans. There are possible anti-trust issues to consider in each case and when it comes to search, contextual or otherwise, my money is on Google. This is not a call to sabotage Facebook by leaving the network either. Each choice you make, has to be your own, guided by your own perception of how you want to create the digital world you will inhabit.

# ■Chapter 4
## The Social Media Addiction

I f I had a dollar for each time I heard someone in a meeting explain how social media is the way forward I would, right now, be writing this book from my own private island in the Maldives instead of having to watch the grey Manchester sky, outside my window.

When it comes to social media there is a trap created by the very words we use. The ability to communicate across the web with virtual strangers, share opinions, news and ideas and have them re-share them has, for better or worse, been called social media marketing and the broader context within which it occurs social media.

Had someone decided to call it "computer generated, digital input through GUI-based communications" the chances are that anything which had to do with it would fall squarely within the domain of an expert and any action anyone, whether a company or individual, undertook would happen only after a carefully laid out process had been created.

Unfortunately this did not happen. We chose, instead, to call online interaction between people and groups of people across the world, social media and any kind of marketing undertaken within that context, social media marketing. The result is that no one wants to admit that they do not 'get' social, it's like asking men to admit to being bad drivers or women to deny that they are sensitive. It simply doesn't happen. As a result I often get to see first-hand social media campaigns and social media plans which are so inept in their planning, let alone their execution, that the only thing which actually saves those who approve them and those who carry them out is the fact that the measure of success of such campaigns is also suitably woolly.

What usually gets to me in these meetings is the needlessness of the problem. Social media is actually designed to work in any context, because, you see, clinical definition notwithstanding, social media really *is* addictive. In order to capitalise on this though you do need to be able to use it in a way which first respects all of its rules and secondly uses the channel in a way which makes the content you post through it, unmissable.

## The online browser syndrome and other social media impulses

I mentioned in the previous chapter that the web makes some issues easier to understand by removing the grey undertones often associated with visual cues in a real-world social setting.

I may, for instance, want to say to my team that they are all asses. That what they thought was a great

Tweet about the waistline increase of the residents of a particular town was, in fact, a PR disaster and they should all be fired. I don't. When I look at them I see people with human failings and home problems, someone who cannot get enough sleep because he has a new addition to the family and someone else who is undergoing a divorce. I know all this, so, instead, I indicate why that particular Tweet may not have been as cleverly targeted as we would like it to be. They would have known by my tone and body language that I was disappointed, that as a team we performed way below the bar and that we would have to do better in future.

Compare this with the online approach to the same problem: "WTF? Who thought that Tweeting about waistlines in a jeans campaign made sense?"

The point is, and it is an important one, that directness, a highly overvalued real-world quality, is actually a prized online commodity and, in many cases, is the default mode of communication in real-time web settings.

Social media is addictive precisely because it gives us something which the real world lacks: it gives us immediacy, direction, a sense of clarity and value as an individual. Whether we are the party executing a social media campaign or some tired, McDonald's manager on the fourth iteration of their career, exhausted from a day's work and wanting to vent some steam, it allows our actions to create a response, which sometimes is immediate.

The paradox of the web has always been that from the isolation of our homes, offices and home offices, we each matter. When we surf the web, although we may do it in total isolation and with the sense that we are anonymous, we also feel that we count. We get the feeling that we are all part of a community of online netizens which also makes us feel that we belong to something and that we are special.

This is an important distinction we will revisit when we examine social media and its application as a marketing tool because it is what makes niche marketing work. For now however we need to examine the dynamics of it at a personal level and see if we can understand exactly what it is that drives this social response in an individual activity, (i.e. surfing the web in isolation) which, technically is anything but social.

We tend to have a picture of the web as comprised of individuals who get online for the single purpose of forming a community to which marketers can market to with precision and economy of effort. Naturally, this picture has about as much truth in it as aerodynamically challenged little pink pigs flying backwards.

We get online because we are looking for something. It may be information for work or to satisfy our curiosity, it might be information for purely entertainment purposes, we may be looking for a product to research or even to buy because we can't face the struggle to find parking downtown. We may be looking for a friend or a sexual partner or a lifelong mate.

I have seen something like this once before. Back in the 70s I was growing up in Australia and CBs were taking off. Usually the preserve of trackers, the success of the TV series, *Dukes of Hazard,* made Citizens' Band radios cool with a hip language all of their own.

The culture which sprung around them was one where school kids and those with time to kill would log onto the air waves and exchange call signs and news with a bunch of faceless people who were known only by their handle. In that universe, now belonging to the last century, 'Iron Maiden' was the call sign of a girl driving a black Ford Mustang who would arrange to meet men on the interstate between Sydney and Brisbane. 'Devil's Son' was a track driver who was on the road six days a week hauling sugarcane up and down the West Coast and 'Circus' was my call sign, a kid who would log on from his bedroom most nights to listen to the crackle of static and the garbled call signs and news being exchanged amongst those who seemed to live lives so much more glamorous and exciting than my own.

The CB phenomenon faded with time as it had no practical value and its reach was limited to a two to five mile radius depending on atmospheric conditions, the frequency used and the best damn CB antenna money could buy. It was my earliest introduction to social media and the impulse to connect, and for me, back then, it created a lasting impact.

The web today is like CB on steroids. Access to anyone is limitless. You can eavesdrop on practically any public conversation you want to and you can form any kind of group you want to or even ask to join one. If CBs were seen as an addictive phenomenon back in the 70s in Australia imagine how the web feels through social connection tools.

Right this moment, as you are reading these words, hundreds of thousands of individuals are meeting potential sexual partners, tens of thousands are approaching someone with a business proposition and millions are browsing, sampling the web with the avid curiosity of the window shopper.

All this activity is made possible because of an inborn drive to connect and share. It's great looking for information for yourself but when you find a great piece it only acquires value if you can also share it with someone. You may be great at processing data in your head, but when that moment of epiphany happens and you have an insight, without an ability to share it, it is like the lone tree falling in the forest. With no one around to hear it, it really makes no sound.

This drive to connect online is the same. Whether you are someone who trawls like a shadow through Facebook profiles looking at party pictures and self-portraits or you are someone who goes from one post to another leaving comments which might inflame someone's sensitivities, it all stems from the same need.

Because that need has been present as long as there are people around, saying that the web created social marketing or social networking is like saying that the web created communities, or even people. The web and its technologies are digital representations of everything we did before in a more private, bigger, faster and more empowering format than ever before.

The moment you understand this, you also begin to 'get' what social is, which means you begin to grasp the implications of social media at a fundamental level which extends beyond mere functionality.

# What exactly is social media?

One of the recurring discussions in my professional life is what exactly is social media. In a way, technically speaking, emails which go back and forth between two people or a group of people about a common subject are a form of social media. I mention this here to indicate the challenge of defining and classifying 'social' in our online activities.

In a way social media is everything we do online, though the more popularly accepted definition has to do with activity which takes place in the online environment of a social network. The real definition of social media however and one which is worthy, for a change, of the additional tack-on of the world 'revolution' is that it is empowerment of the individual at the expense of the system.

For much of the 20th century (and all the centuries before it) everything we had set up as business was mirrored upon the command and control structure of the military model. It's no accident that many former military men found great homes in corporations, after their army career was over. Business, was set up in ways where people were subordinate to processes, there to make sure that the process itself took place. This model of governance and business is one which is limited by nature. It works in times of crisis (and even this is arguable) because it enables large companies to move fast and make difficult decisions quickly but it also uses up people as 'cannon fodder' and has a record of attrition equal to any war. For a start it made us accept the model of downsizing as a business strategy. In this context the management of the company, acting in the role of an army commander, make decisions which need to be followed and, just like in a battle, should they prove to go wrong, it is the hard-working staff who, just like soldiers, have to pay the 'ultimate sacrifice' and lose their jobs, while management gets rewarded with another try (and often lauded for making 'tough' decisions).

It does not take much insight to understand that this model awes as much to logic as the Mad Hatter's Tea Party. While on the surface of it, it appears to make perfect sense the dynamics under which it operates which allow a command and control structure to function in a battlefield, are different to that of a real war and this leads to all sorts of inconsistencies: We, for instance, reward performance and yet a poor management decision may well result in hundreds if not thousands of workers who had worked hard to execute it, lose their jobs, in essence punishing their performance, while the ones who managed them, whose performance ought to be punished, usually get rewarded.

We prize creativity, initiative and commitment to the company yet reward unquestioning loyalty which best follows internal protocols and chain-of-command and does not rock the boat.

The traditional command and control model worked well enough as long as people were willing to be 'corporate soldiers', valuing loyalty and obedience above all else (giving the term 'company man' a bad name in the process) but it was inevitable that at some point it would begin to break down.

The first cracks appeared when Black Monday in 1987 led to a global stock market crash which wiped out, in some cases, as much as 50% of the paper value of many companies, necessitating the beginning of the culture of change which has not stopped to our day.

The recession which followed in the opening years of the 90s only accelerated the rate of change and the rapid advance of technology only made change occur faster. With each round of change the old system faltered more and more, requiring greater efforts to fix it along the way, until it became obvious that it was broken beyond repair.

Social media, by degrees, is forcing a change in the way business is structured. The new model that is replacing the old Command and Control system is one of network management. Put simply, things are now changing so fast that the rigid mechanistic structures of the past are simply failing. It has actually become harder to be productive in a big organization, economies of scale are reversing themselves in command and control environments. And in these new organizations that are networks of capable individuals who have great communications tools, leadership and the ability to create cooperative, synergistic solutions emerge as more important than the traditional, top-down command structure.

Hierarchy, process and automation in networks are returning to their proper place as tools that support human efficiency and capability. Rather than the 20th century model of people existing to keep the processes running, we are now flipping it around so that processes exist to support people. Processes and automation amplify human capability. Importantly, there is another profound amplifier of human capability and that is other humans, which is where collaboration and synergy come in. The focus on collaboration fuelled by radically improved communication and the internet which is rapidly becoming a prosthetic tool aiding memory, helping in the storage and retrieval of data and providing new tools to connect individuals and help them collaborate better, is dramatically changing how we think about organizational structure, efficiency, learning and innovation.

It is hard to imagine, for instance, a social media campaign which can work both cost-effectively and correctly if it has to be micromanaged every step of the way.

The inversion of the old models is necessitating the building of trust as an integral part of the equation. Whereas in the past a company would rigidly manage its image, deliver everything from a tightly controlled top-down approach with a unified message being spread, irrespective of whether it really was true or not, the new open model entrusts this image to a company's customers, enabling them to claim ownership of it and become its brand ambassadors, when they believe in it, and its fiercest critics, when they do not.

This is a brave, dynamic, organic model which acknowledges that a business, any business, puts the human element first, and enters into an unwritten contract with its customers which essentially says to them: "We both want the same thing: to give you the best service/product/information your money can buy. You want to get it cost-effectively and we want to make some money so we can continue to serve you. Now how can we achieve this to our mutual benefit?"

This kind of collaboration between customer and business would have been unthinkable and prohibitively expensive in the pre-social media age. Today it is unthinkable, to me, to see a company which does not operate like this.

Now, I know what you are thinking. Giving up power is difficult. Entrusting feckless customers is difficult. Social media however is easy, right? All you need is a Twitter account, a Google Plus profile and a Facebook Page and you are set to take over the social media world, right?

I will give you an example of a company which made the classic mistake of believing that having the tools, rather than knowing how to use them, was the important thing, while in every other aspect it retained its command and control structure.

I have a Blackberry. I have had one since 2006. I love the push technology its email service gives you, the fact that Blackberry servers are secure and the ease with which I can connect to my email accounts from anywhere and be kept in the loop with information I need, no matter where I am in the world.

On Monday 10th October 2011 the Blackberry service suffered an outage across Europe which affected 30% of their clients. By midday the outage had spread with more than 40% affected. Because this is the real-time web age, the moment the outage made itself felt, Blackberry users went on Twitter to check out what was happening and share the issue with other users.

As the outage was Europe wide and had begun to affect some Latin American countries #Blackberry became a trending topic on Twitter within hours.

From a PR point of view this is a potential disaster in the making. RIM, the Canadian company which owns the Blackberry brand in 2011 had seen its ambitious tablet project, the Blackberry Playbook, which had been widely anticipated to be an iPad killer, flop. More than that it has become the third company in a race dominated by just two players in the smartphone market: Google and its Android OS and Apple with its iPhone.

Logic dictates that when you are fighting for your life the last thing you want to do is to appear to be locked into a communication mode which belongs to the past.

Blackberry tries to be progressive. It has a Twitter account which it uses to provide technical tips for its phones and to answer the questions its smartphone users have so you'd think they would have their finger on the pulse of social media. Yet over three hours later their tech team @BlackBerryHelp, oblivious to the social media disaster they were facing, were adding fuel to the fire by cheerfully chirping from their account: "Hey #teamblackberry happy Monday everyone! Hope you all had a great weekend we are back to answer your questions stay tuned for answers."

You can see that's bad, right? But it gets worse. Three and a half hours after the outage had started and had become a trending topic on Twitter Blackberry had still not officially acknowledged it. Even worse, in the UK which is one of Blackberry's largest markets, the spokeswoman for the company announced that an official statement would be made a little later that day.

Twitter account notwithstanding if Blackberry had wanted to announce to the world that it was an entrenched command and control company whose communications structure belonged to the 20th century instead of the 21st, it could not have done a better job.

I was not alone in deciding that day to switch smartphones in the full expectation that Blackberry would soon be either a spent force, tying me down to software and devices which would be out-of-date the day they were released, or offering services which could not be relied upon.

It did not have to be this way of course. Even with a PR disaster in their hands this could have been a golden opportunity for Blackberry to step up and take control of it, explaining itself, creating that connection which even irate users, disgruntled with the service's failure for a few hours, would find endearing and which would help it win that all vital "hearts and minds" game which turns customers into brand ambassadors ready to fight in your corner.

This kind of approach of course requires the company to have a social media mind. It must understand that Twitter and Google Plus and Facebook are not channels to release standardised responses in and press releases. It had to actually 'get' that in order to use them properly it had to have an internal communication system in place which kept its hard working tech team in the loop so that they knew of service issues before they broke.

Instead, that day, I and countless others saw a corporation which asked for my custom while it did nothing to gain it. It expected me to buy its products and use its services because they had a cool logo and had once had a reputation as the smartphone kings.

If social media sounds unforgiving it is because it is. It lends new life to the old showbiz creed of "any publicity is good publicity" and it provides the opportunity to truly foster a dialogue and create meaningful online relationships. Had Blackberry, that day, stepped up, seized the opportunity and communicated so clearly and with such finesse that it made everyone wish they owned a Blackberry (and people always understand, once they cool down, that tech disasters happen from time to time and no one is immune to them), they would have gained hundreds of thousands of dollars, even millions, worth of publicity and, quite possibly, thousands of new customers who would have gone out to check their products.

Instead they managed to project the image of a global company that keeps Canadian hours, sitting in a corporate banker from which they issue official Press Releases. With the eyes and ears of the world upon them, all that could be seen on Twitter were the hundreds of thousands of messages such as this one: "iPhone users say 'I told you so!' #Blackberry".

## Social media demands responsiveness

Before we look at the practicalities of social media marketing I will close with an example which exemplifies how a social media mind thinks. When Toyota first introduced Lexus in 1989, in the US, it was in direct competition with BMW and Mercedes, two brands which had an entrenched market share and a similar ticket price.

Lexus' launch started with an apparent glitch. Based upon two customer complaints Lexus initiated a voluntary recall of all 8,000 LS 400s sold up to that point. In a sweeping 20-day operation which replaced the parts on all affected vehicles, Lexus sent technicians to pick up, repair, and return cars to customers free of charge, and also flew in personnel and rented garage space for owners in remote locations.

No one has ever said what the action cost, but the decisiveness it revealed behind it, the promptness of that response and the quality of service it revealed, created a stark contrast with the slightly haughty attitude of BMW and Mercedes dealerships and was instrumental in creating a buzz around wine bars and in the Press which was began to create the air of affordable exclusivity which Lexus needed to successfully break into the market.

Had Twitter been around back then, my guess is that the Lexus brand would have grown even faster. The example, shows however that you do not need to have a specific channel in place in order to use social media tactics which help you succeed. You just need to have an awareness of the potential offered by social media and possess the kind of creative, social media thinking which helps you take advantage of it.

Today we are awash with tools which help spread the message marketing managers want to send and tools which help analyse its effectiveness. All this data requires someone to check it, understand it and make decisions on the fly. Command and control structures here hinder, rather than help. They create bottlenecks which overwhelm the system and cause it to crash.

It is only by developing a social media mindset that social media, at any level can be successfully tackled.

If you are ready to make the transition from a Command and Control system of management to a network management one, the characteristics which mark the Social Media Mind are easy enough to develop:

‣ **Identity** – You may be an individual or you may be part of a global corporation with hundreds of thousands of employees. If, however, you cannot talk to those you are trying to reach with a voice which allows them to get a sense of personality and who you are, you are only going to run into hot water sooner or later. Before social media marketing came into play to the extent we see today, Chief Marketing Officers would make their teams create Marketing Personas to better help them visualise the ideal customer. The person they are supposed to be addressing with their marketing messages and adverts. Today of course they have direct access to customers and their personalities which makes the very notion of a marketing persona for social media, outmoded. There is a need however for a marketing persona in reverse, creating, in essence a 'person' who signifies the brand or the company and what it stands for.

‣ **Voice** – This goes hand-in-hand with identity. If you do not know how you should sound when you communicate with those you want to reach then it is unlikely that you will manage to strike the right tone you need in order to really help them get to know you. Remember the web is devoid of visual and aural nuances. This means that what you post and how you post it. How you choose to respond to questions and even inflammatory remarks helps those who read it form an idea of how you sound and who you are.

‣ **Openness** – Social media is about being as honest as possible. In the old Command and Control business structure managers were judged by how quickly they could bury mistakes and pretend they'd never happened. In the new world of social media companies, corporations and individuals need to be quick to admit to making mistakes, dropping the ball on crucial issues and failing to address basic concepts. By the same token they also need to be quick to make reparations, show they have taken action and actually establish that when mistakes happen they are never wilful and that client and supplier actually want the same thing: a smooth transaction and a feeling that they have done a great job. For most corporations this is a massive culture change. Admitting you are wrong used to be seen as weakness and, in the old-world thinking, this was giving competitors an advantage. This is no longer valid though. In social media people understand that it is still people who provide the service and that their role is to make it work. By establishing a direct connection, even during a crisis, with the customers they are maintaining loyalty and support and forging relationships which are harder to break.

‣ **Trust** – Because social media is about relationships, albeit online ones, within a context which is defined by a service or a product, it is all about creating a sense of trust in suppliers and consumers alike. This is not as complicated as it may at first sound. The pre-social media notion of generating trust in the clients of a company involved fancy packaging, glossy office building exteriors, an investment in appearances. There was an implicit assumption there that such things impressed consumers who would then transfer that good impression to the company's products and services. We have really gone way beyond this. YouTube videos, for instance, shot on laptop cams with grainy quality and poor lighting, go viral because their appeal is real. The rise of web-savvy, PR-aware consumers has removed the effectiveness of the old style of marketing. Companies which get social media are quick to put, in its place, a genuine dialogue which when boiled down to its essence goes along these lines: "We want to sell to you, but we do not want you to buy and disappear. We want you to buy from us and keep on buying. We want you to tell your friends about us and we want them to be so impressed that they tell their friends. We know that the only way to achieve this is for us to let you know that what we do is more than a job. It is a calling. We want to be the best possible in our field. Because we want you to be totally happy with what we offer, we are on the same page. We will listen carefully to what you want and provide not what we want to sell but what is the best possible solution to your needs. If things go wrong, which sometimes they do, we will move heaven and earth to set them right. Although you are a customer we treat you the way ourselves would like to be treated if we were customers."

This kind of dialogue requires guts. First a company has to be quick to understand what it is that truly makes it special. Then it has to work hard to find, before its customers do, where it falls short of the mark and fix it. Then it has to trust everyone within the company to work to that standard by creating a culture which truly values employees and their work. Finally it has to trust its customers to take the message further afield and, when things go wrong, understand how well the service worked to fix it, and take that message further afield. In retrospect the old way of doing things appears to be the easier, cheaper solution which is why so many companies are resistant to changing. Unfortunately, there really is no going back to the ways of the past.

› **Ingenuity** – Given an infinite amount of money and infinite time any company can become the best one in the known universe. The thing is that if your company really had that kind of money it would not need to be in business and you would not have a job. This brings us down to the way things are done normally in any business environment where any given project, including customer service and social media marketing is on a limited budget, with hardly any manpower and almost no time to do anything in. You really need to be clever and, to use a way too-overused phrase, be prepared to think outside the box, in order to achieve it. Social media is still new and constantly evolving. You should be prepared to evolve with it. More than that, working in this field requires that you find ways to take it further. At the end of the day social media marketing is all about that essential element of connecting and, because people are always different, and connections are made in many different ways, finding new means to achieve it should be part of the job description.

# ■Chapter 5
## The Social Business Edge

T he word 'revolution' is an easy one to come by in almost every sphere today. We live in a media-orientated age where the channels vying for our attention are multiplying, just as our attention spans become shorter. Under the circumstances the media (mostly the Press) can hardly be blamed for resorting to cheap tactics to grab our eyeballs long enough for whatever message they have written to be read. The word 'revolution' is one of them. We are experiencing, invariably, an information revolution, a robotics revolution, a communication revolution and a social media revolution.

As a matter of fact, had one of our distant relatives from the far future come back in time to meet us they would have to be forgiven if they suddenly felt that we live in revolutionary times where anything we did in the past is under threat and everything we do today is new and, as yet, disorganized.

I do not dislike the word, of course, but I am not a great fan of usage that's loose and free and is done just so someone can catch my attention. Revolution, in my book, is a term which applies to a total breakdown of systems which have existed for a long time, a sweeping away of the established practices and the setting up of something which is ideologically new or at least new in principle as well as application. The change we see in the online world and where the online world meets the offline one, is not sufficiently traumatic (or even dramatic) to deserve that, but it can, in all honesty, be better called 'evolution'.

In truth, what we are experiencing is the evolution of processes, as we take practices and beliefs we applied in the offline world, modify them to suit new scales of application and put them to work for us, online.

Social media marketing is one of them and it's changing the way we do business. Evolution, of course, does not mean it is any less painful than revolution. If anything, evolution can be even more painful and confusing. In the former we are subconsciously prepared to experience discomfort, confusion and upsets. In the latter, we rarely are. And yet, it is evolution which has the most growing pain as processes which have worked for a long time now need to be re-assessed, modified, adapted, tried and assessed again.

It's little wonder companies fail to 'get' social media marketing. The average company, to survive, has to rely on processes and processes, generally speaking, require a command and control structure where someone is in charge and they all answer, ultimately, to that person.

## The social media trap

If you are in business the economy is always tough. If things are going great your competitors are also surging ahead and you need to keep abreast of them. If things are 'tough' then the pressure to adopt new marketing channels and change the current ones you have is suffocating.

In just one short year, social media marketing went from being the preserve of web-savvy marketers who could see that eyeballs on a brand or a product offered the potential to eventually increase market share, to being the darling of the press and almost every company 'out there' who suddenly felt the need to jump on the bandwagon.

This also created a culture where social media marketing is something suddenly being offered by the world and his brother as online marketers of every description hurried to jump on before the train left the station. This is exactly where the trap is usually sprung.

Social media is so popular because it appears easy to do. After all there is no rocket science involved in putting hashtags on Twitter, getting some 'Likes' on Facebook or seeing the +1 counter rise on Google Plus. Now, here's the catch, even finely tuned social media marketing campaigns, carried out by experts, provide no hard correlation between social media marketing and sales. The number of these is finite and relatively rare.

The majority of media marketing campaigns I see are either ill-conceived or poorly executed, or both. Take, for instance, the very recent and very public social media disaster of the Ragu social media campaign which used a video with last-century, defining, stereotypes to launch a Twitter campaign (because Ragu does social media, right?) which spammed the Twitter accounts of males there and raised the ire of internet marketers. The culmination of it was a grassroots

Twitter counter-campaign which centred on the sentiment: 'Ragu hates Dads'.

Obviously they did not intend to create that reaction. But as any journalist worth his salt knows and as any social media manager who understands what they are doing will tell you, every reaction is good and it creates an opportunity to win 'hearts and minds'. Ragu, to stick with the current example, blew even this opportunity by accusing in their Tweets, critical posts as "lacking balance". When called to task over it they simply shut up.

What all this illustrates is that what is apparently easy to do in terms of execution, actually is not. I consider strumming an acoustic guitar a fairly easy thing to do also, but going from that strumming to actually producing the kind of tune which will make people around me stop what they are doing and take notice and then put their hands together and clap when I am done takes finesse, talent, sensitivity and a lot of hard work.

Social media marketing is no exception. Funnily enough I saw the same Bell curve of popularity take off with SEO at the beginning of 2008 with just about anybody out there offering "to SEO your website" and it is only when we got down to needing meaningful results and bottom-line orientated numbers that the inevitable shakeout began to happen.

Social media marketing will follow the same development curve. To say that it is difficult to quantify is no excuse. What social media marketers need to do is see the difficulties as a challenge. The recently announced real-time Google Analytics is able to address at least part of this issue by providing real-time correlation between social media marketing initiatives and website traffic, the behaviour of which can be tracked precisely.

The infatuation of the Press with social media is going to continue for the immediate future but the shake-up will happen and only marketers who understand how to deliver real value and measure it will stand any chance of success, when this occurs.

Being forewarned means being forearmed. So how do you make sure your company and business avoids the social media trap, where, on paper, you tick all the boxes but the results you get are not the ones you expect?

There are a few simple guidelines you can implement:

‣ **Decide what you want to achieve in social media.** This is basic and yet many companies forget to even consider it. If there is no simple, clear mission statement which can summarise the goal then much of the social media marketing effort will be dissipated in unnecessary actions. In my time as social media advisor I have seen company managers come out of four hour meetings with the aim to: "Reposition the company as the main supplier of an aggressively priced product in a B2B environment consistent with current market values." If you just did a double-take reading this, you are not the only one. They could have much more easily said: "We sell wholesale at mind-bogglingly low prices" and got it over with, but even that would have been wrong within a social media marketing message. In a social media environment selling happens almost as a by-product, an aside to the primary task which is getting people to know your company and your company getting to know and understand its potential customers.

‣ **Work out a voice for your company.** How you communicate is every bit as important as what you communicate. The real-life example I gave above perfectly illustrates the point. Company executives and company owners think like company executives and company owners and in their heads there are reports and report-speak which goes on all the time. Social media marketing, on the other hand, is more like every day conversation. Those who notice what you post online in a social media environment respond to things they can understand immediately and which will catch their attention. Well, that simple message needs to be consistent not just when it markets (that's easy enough to do) but also when it replies to questions, responds to other comments and generally creates an impression of what your company is really like.

‣ **Make social media part of your company's DNA.** This is as simple to say as it is difficult to execute: in order to succeed in social media marketing you need to make social media awareness part of every level of your company in a feedback loop that supplies content to your social media team and feedback from the social media team to all other parts of the company.

‣ **Create a strategy not a practice.** There is a significant difference. Social media implemented without strategic vision to guide it almost always occurs in a vacuum. Real problems can arise from a social media channel that works independently of what other initiatives, issues or responses exist in other parts of the company. The example of Blackberry we saw is a classic case in point. By perfectly executing their job as they were supposed to, those manning the Blackberry service Twitter account managed to damage the company and its reputation by making it appear disconnected, uncaring and insensitive, and all because that strategic vision was not in place. To succeed, again, social media marketing must neatly dovetail into all the other company marketing efforts. Do you use email marketing? Link your social media services to it. Mention in your social media services that your HTML Newsletter has just gone out and provide a link for those who want to, to either go and see it online (and register) or go and register for the next one. Do you use offline marketing? Link it to your online efforts and mention online what you do too. Social media marketing is not some weird, wonderful way of marketing which allows you to disregard all the rules of marketing and still see results. You need to create reinforcing loops so that each piece of marketing you do feeds off, and possibly reinforces, the waves of what has gone before and, in turn, makes everything which will come after, easier.

▸ **Tell a story.** The best illusionists in the business no longer do magic tricks. Instead they tell a story which has components which completely boggle the mind. A piece disappears here, something else appears somewhere else. A new part of the puzzle comes into effect, something breaks which shouldn't and magically recreates itself. Piecemeal these are cheap tricks. Pull them altogether in one cohesive whole and you have a story which is compelling, magical and greater than the sum of its parts. Do the same thing in your marketing and here's what happens: A. Your audience becomes enamoured. B. Your audience grows. C. The story you tell has a chance of becoming viral. D. Your 'message' is better understood.

> **Measure effectiveness**. The single, greatest complaint social media clients have is that there are no hard-and-fast results in social media marketing. The biggest complaint social media marketers voice is that it is difficult to measure the effectiveness of social media marketing efforts. Both are right, but this is no justification. While it is true that there are no *traditional* means of measuring the effectiveness of marketing through social media this does not mean that there cannot be devised ways to measure marketing efforts. Each situation is unique, but just like offline, traditional mail mailshot marketing is carried out in ways which are designed to be measurable. It is inconceivable that we can, as marketers, find ways to measure the effectiveness of mailshots based on nothing more than stupid paper and we cannot measure the effectiveness of social media efforts when we have at our disposal a variety of incredibly detailed and intelligent ways to track online consumer behaviour.

> **Refine technique**. Consider this simple example. You meet a friend in the street you haven't seen for some time and start exchanging pleasantries. You say 'how are you?' – the usual, trite interactions, as a matter of fact and he suddenly announces that his wife was killed in a car crash just a day before. Do you: A. Carry on the conversation telling him about your day and the problems you had or B. Stop cold and offer your most sincere sympathy and ask if there is anything you can do. C. Do an about turn and run away. It's a no-brainer, right? The ease with which you adjust your responses and interactions in a two-way, face-to-face

conversation, apparently, must not easily transfer to the two-way conversation that takes place in a social network setting, otherwise how can we explain the rigid, non-responsive way of 'communicating' most companies put in place today? Apart from the fact that now, it is also becoming inexcusable to market the same way to Facebook followers (different tastes, interactions and demographics) as you do to Google+, or Twitter, having a one-way rigid way of communicating is downright criminal. It is true that an overlap in demographics and even audience in social networks may allow for similar messages to be posted, the way you present them, however, should be tailored to the etiquette and tropes of each social media platform.

‣ **Stay current**. Nothing spoils social media marketing faster than an inability to respond to current trends. Imagine this Twitter trend background: A flood in Philadelphia which leaves thousands homeless and starts a Tweet avalanche. Provide Tweets or social network marketing that shows insensitivity to this and you have set yourself up for a fall, particularly if you are criticised and cannot respond properly because you are unaware of the context behind the criticism.

‣ **Listen and respond**. You are actively marketing your brand, your company name and your products or services in a social media network setting. There is no excuse for not carrying out regular vanity searches, setting up Google alerts and monitoring social networks for what's being said about you. And listening is not enough. You also need to have a complete contingency plan in hand so your social media team knows how to respond when it comes to dealing with social media comments which may be less than complimentary.

▸ **Be authentic**. Of all the things you have to do in your social media marketing and in the fashioning of your new social media mind, being authentic in what you present online is probably the hardest thing to pull off. It's hard because, realistically, you cannot do it. This is what every business wants: money from its customers who then go away saying only great things about the business and do not bother it again unless it is to bring in more business. This is what most businesses get: customers who want 'above and beyond' in every aspect of the product and service, with a transaction weighed in their favour and everything offered as cheaply as possible. It is understandably difficult to be completely yourself online and, probably, it is not even advisable. But in order to succeed you do need to become more transparent with as few layers as possible between who you are and what you do, as a business.

## How to be more authentic

Being authentic is not new. When I was active at corporate level I was lucky enough (and it was luck) to become part of a team which put this to work across a workforce totalling over 150,000 members of staff at the time. It gave me insights which I have since worked into an approach which I call Truth Marketing. The danger with any kind of approach like this is that you have to have a conscience (in the corporation I worked in we actually invested in independent personnel whose main role was to help keep us 'honest' and true to our professed ideals – a move which was both costly and unprecedented in terms of corporate initiatives) or corporate expediency will erode even the best of intentions.

In order for 'authentic' and 'real' to work in marketing you have to invest part of yourself in it. I say only part because to invest everything is to lose focus of the issue and probably create more problems than you solve. As readers, for instance, we really want to know a little of what makes our favourite authors tick, so that it allows us to connect with them at a deeper level than just that of work creators, but we probably do not want to know all their foibles, where they buy their milk, if they are having an argument with their partner and whether they agonise over which brand of deodorant to buy. That is so real and so authentic perhaps that it demythologises things a little too much and somehow deflates the experience.

We are back to our wishful thinking and knowledge. We all want 'heroes' of some kind and we all then want to know them and (at a proverbial level) buy them a drink. A writer who spends 20 hours glued to their keyboard because the idea they are pursuing in their writing is so compelling fires us up. The ability to then connect with that writer over a social network setting and exchange some pleasantries or even discuss that idea, honestly and openly, is something few of us can resist. In that discussion, we fancy, we let the writer know how we appreciate (or not) their thoughts on the subject and in the exchange connect with them, the same way we might have at a bar, over a beer. In their responses and interaction we also get to know them a little.

That part of 'authentic' and 'real', actually works. The writer gets to really connect with those who read what he writes and those who read what he writes deliver invaluable insights and feedback back to the writer in a setting which helps both. All, provided, of course, the writer does not become defensive and hide behind a façade (in which case the 'authentic' suddenly becomes its opposite) or that they do not become too relaxed and dismiss the issue with 'hey bub. Just read the work, I don't even know myself half of its implications', which would prove that our statue does have feet of clay, after all.

## Data, damned data!

In October 2011 IBM released the findings of a research study it carried out between February and June 2011 where it interviewed, face-to-face 1,700 CMOs about their perceptions and use of social media marketing. The results were as shocking as they were revealing.

A mere 26 percent of chief marketing officers track blogs and just 40 percent track any online communications, while 82 percent still rely on traditional market research to shape marketing strategies. In other words, while living in the bright glare of the social media age most CMOs prefer doing things in the dark or with their eyes shut.

Why? There is always a reason we eschew the use of new technology and it has little to do with our fear of change or our unwillingness to embrace different ways of working. In social media marketing, just like in search engine optimization (SEO) I come across the same chestnut: data, or rather a surfeit of data and our inability to process it in a way which makes sense to us.

While some 82 percent of the CMOs said they planned to increase their use of social media over the next 3-5 years, the problem was beautifully highlighted when one of the respondents, when asked, said: "The perfect solution is to serve each consumer individually. The problem? There are 7 billion of them."

The fact is that when Twitter alone generates some 200 million Tweets per day. YouTube can generate tens of thousands of views and comments, Google Plus can give you hundreds of interactions and you can get thousands of Likes and shares from Facebook, all on a single post you have made, the challenge is to separate the 'signal' from the 'noise' and actually understand what is happening in terms of your marketing and brand.

How do we deal with all this data?

IBM, the masters of re-invention, who survived a life-threatening moment in the 90s only to emerge stronger, leaner and with a clearer sight of where they were heading than most companies at the time, believe that the answer lies in automation. At some point companies will need automated processes like that of Google Analytics, which will be capable of showing them where and how their social data is used, who it reaches and how they re-use it and have embarked on an aggressive acquisition campaign of companies with the technology required to make this happen.

Purists believe that social media data is best analysed on a one-to-one basis, much like the dialogue which takes place in a social media channel needs to be carried out in an intensely personal way in order to be effective.

Right now there is no ready-made shortcut and though the integration of social media channels like Twitter and Facebook might save some valuable time and provide a stop-gap measure while you get your communication strategy worked out, in the long run they will begin to signal that you really do not care and that you treat social media marketing as a channel which you must employ without clearly understanding how.

That kind of approach will work, just, only as long as your business is working OK. The moment things begin to wobble your lack of preparation or indeed, your lack of strategy will show immediately and cause the kind of backfiring that has seen the tarnishing of so many major brands.

# ■Chapter 6
## Social Business Strategies

No paradigm shift ever happens (and arguably does not even begin) without there being some money in it for somebody. The telegraph, the Press, the telephone, television and the internet are all life changing inventions. Each, in its time, changed the way we communicate, altered the way we connect, helped speed up the rate at which information travels, helped create a common frame of reference, levelled local and cultural barriers and created cultures and global outlooks which were no longer informed by the parochial, the tribal, the superstitious view. None of them would have happened if there was no money to be made somewhere.

This is not a jaded view of the world. It's a fact that we all have to eat and, for better or worse, we are drawn to activities which provide the best return for our efforts. If the benefit of carrier pigeons from an economic point of view made sense the telegraph would never have taken off, never mind how great an invention or breakthrough it was.

In the 16th century Feudal Japan became the only nation in history to turn its back on the gun which, up to that point, they had adopted from the West and vastly improved in quality, accuracy and rate of fire. This incredible decision which was imposed on 29 August 1588 by the peasant-turned-Shogun, Hidéyoshi, lasted 265 years until the arrival of Commodore Matthew Perry on July 14, 1853 at Uraga Harbor, which essentially marked the re-opening of Japan and the end of its self-imposed isolation.

Up to that point in its history the Japanese gunsmiths had taken gun-making to technological levels which surpassed those of the West and the gun had been instrumental in helping Hidéyoshi unite Japan under a strong central government. The reasons he abolished it was that there were more financial, cultural, political and even ideological interests tied to its abolition than its continued presence. And they were so strong that the ban held for more than two and a half centuries.

When it became expedient again for Japan to re-arm itself, open its borders and embrace the gun it did so wholeheartedly and without hesitation because, again, it made more sense politically, financially and culturally to have guns again than not to.

The point is that while at an individual and even, occasionally at a tribal or group level, we may make decisions and engage in behaviour which does not easily stand the test of logic, from a more removed perspective the need to eat, survive and thrive is driven by such remorseless logic that the whole (whether that is a country, a society or a federation) progresses along paths which are strictly logical in their course.

History has shown this in the oddest ways. Ancient Sparta, the world's only and foremost war nation, managed to create a warrior class out of its citizenry, fashioning a city-state which was ran like a boot camp and having a society which constantly lived under the threat of war, because it made more sense to run it like this than not to. This way of life created more money, more time and more resources than any other option they might have considered.

The French Revolution some 3,000 years later was also governed, in its dynamic, by the same core reasoning which drove the creation of Sparta and the isolation of Japan from the West.

The point is, to completely popularise the argument, that unless there is a *Jerry Maguire* "Show Me The Money" argument in any kind of development, it is unlikely to catch on, no matter how hard anyone pushes.

Social media is the same. Its adoption is driven by the sense that there is money to be made in it and from it. Businesses, desperate to drive down marketing costs in the 21st century and create that elusive kind of customer: the loyal consumer, are clasping at anything and everything, which promises that it might help them do just that.

The urge to jump on the bandwagon is driven by desperation rather than conviction and it has produced some elegantly irrational arguments: I have lost count of the number of boardroom meetings in which I was present and the argument that was floated was one of numbers. It went along these lines (and you can fill in your own figures) "x number of people are there. X use it on a daily basis. Our efforts will be seen by x." X, of course, as any fifth grader knows both marks the spot on the pirate maps and stands for the unknown quantity in maths equations and, in the case of social media marketing, frequently stands for both.

The boardroom meetings featuring the argument invariably end with the sentiment of "we must fish where the fish are" and then everyone usually turns to me to take over and explain how this must now be achieved.

If I also did not suffer from the need to eat I would, invariably, at that stage take my leave and go and spend some constructive time with my family and friends. The need to ensure that there is food beyond the next moment drives me to explain, in simple, logical terms the same things I will explain in the next section.

## Social media marketing isn't working

Sixty-two percent of online retailers say their return on investment is either unaffected by social media or that the benefits remain unclear. This is according to Forrester Research's, *The State of Retailing Online 2011: Marketing, Social & Mobile*, which was released in May 2011, to members of Shop.org, the online retail division of the National Retail Federation.

For those of us working in SEO and social marketing the research results were hardly a surprise. After all we have seen the likes of this before with SEO which underwent a period of 'giving uncertain returns' when compared to traditional marketing and advertising only for the proverbial penny to finally drop and SEO to become the core activity around which online marketing revolves.

The last report to come out of Agency GroupM and Comscore stated that 58% of consumers start the purchase process with search, outpacing company websites (24%) and social media (18%). This puts search at the heart of any company marketing worth its salt and begs the obvious question: 'why is social marketing not working?'.

The glib answer is, it is working but you just can't see it. You're reading this however because you want something a little more than glib so let's go and explore the real reasons behind figures designed to sink the heart of any company social marketing manager.

**Social Media Marketing and what it does**: Back at marketing school the first lesson learnt was that word-of-mouth publicity was worth its weight in platinum. This personal approach to marketing was always super-difficult to achieve and provided the best conversions in terms of time and effort spent. After all, who amongst us has not considered making a purchase of something just on the recommendation of a friend?

It is a small leap of logic to go from that personal approach to the digital equivalent which is social marketing. The logic is irrefutable enough to convince us that it has to work and that's exactly where the problem lies.

Social marketing, for all its seemingly similar approach to personal word-of-mouth publicity is not the same thing. Setting up Facebook profiles and recruiting thousands of 'friends' does not automatically mean that the moment you recommend something those who see it will rush out to buy it. Having a Twitter account which is read by tens of thousands of followers does not automatically give you the ability to sway their purchasing decisions.

The reason this is not happening is because the marketing we put in place on social networks is perfectly logical but the mechanism (for lack of a better word) we employ when we make a purchasing decision is anything but. Consumers buy through emotion. We relate to brands based on how they make us feel and we buy things because of the way they affect the way we see ourselves.

This emotional approach to buying goes so deep as to extend to, even, basic purchases such as food and coffee. The reason we go to a Wall Mart or Costco, the reason we buy from Sears or Waitrose, the choices which make us patrons of a particular chain of department stores or an eclectic upmarket establishment are purely emotional, restrained only by a basic principle: what is in our wallet.

When we understand this we also understand that Social Media Marketing, in its present form, is less about making people buy or even making them think about buying and more about fostering the kind of relationship which may lead to them to start thinking about buying.

In short, although Social Media Marketing may appear, at first glance to be the digital equivalent of that all-powerful word-of-mouth publicity, in reality it is really nothing more than a digital handshake, an introduction of sorts. Just like in the real world an introduction has to go through the stages of someone shaking your hand, finding out something about you, getting to know you a little bit better and then, finally, taking your recommendation to buy something, so does social marketing on the web need to go through the same process.

**Social Media Marketing is an Introduction**: This makes every effort you put in place on social marketing networks nothing more than a handshake with the potential to lead to something more. The reason most social marketing today is perceived not to work is because those who apply it do so thinking they are selling. They are not. They are becoming better known and if the process of getting to know them better is one which introduces products and services which have real foundations and solid logic behind them, then, it shall lead to sales, brand awareness and eventually a bigger share of the market. Not before.

As you may imagine, the moment I explain this, the next question they hit me with is, "Can it be made to work for us?". The answer here is yes. Social Media Marketing can be made to work for any type of business, from the one-man outfit to the 250,000 strong corporate group provided there is a clarity in the targets which need to be achieved and the implementation of the social media campaign.

There are very specific elements which help make any social media marketing successful. Before we even look at them it'll be prudent to look at some examples of social media marketing campaigns which have produced results. These will form the common frame of reference against which any which do not will make more sense.

# Social media success stories

**#1 – Virgin America**: Virgin America (Twitter handle: @VirginAmerica)

Virgin America has managed to create a powerful following through a potent mix of business promotions and social conscience. It uses Promoted Trends and Promoted Tweets to announce low fares and give back to a great cause with Stand Up To Cancer

In 2007, Virgin sought to redefine the customer experience for air travellers by launching Virgin America in the United States. It gained competitive market share by humanizing its brand through fun and tech- forward amenities such as custom-designed mood-lit cabins, leather seats, video touch-screens, power outlets and WiFi at every seat — all for an attractive fare.

As part of the strategy of amplifying the positive word-of-mouth about its unique service, the airline stressed the importance of social media because of its high-touch customer service approach. It created an active community on Twitter, primarily using it to communicate relevant company news, promotional airfares and guest care concerns. Virgin America wanted to reach a broader digital audience with its low fares however. The challenge was to do so without losing the positive brand association that its customers were now familiar with.

To achieve this, Virgin America partnered with Stand Up To Cancer to launch a one-day flash sale exclusively on Twitter called the "Fly Forward, Give Back" campaign. Fares started at $49 with $5 going to the charitable cancer organization with each booking (up to a total of $50,000).

The airline used a Promoted Trend with the hashtag #FlyFwdGiveBack to broadcast the sale to a broader audience on Twitter. Trends are featured prominently next to a user's timeline and reflect what the hottest topics are at the moment on Twitter. A Promoted Trend is ideally placed at the top of these trending topics to amplify a conversation on Twitter.

Virgin America also ran a Promoted Tweet campaign during the sale. Abby Lunardini, Vice President of Corporate Communications at Virgin America once explained the strategy: "As an early adopter, we've had a lot of success with Twitter's other beta products in naturally amplifying the ongoing conversations we already see, so we were excited to see the results of Promoted Tweets together with a Promoted Trend. We targeted our Promoted Tweets to our followers so while the Promoted Trend drove mass awareness, the Promoted Tweet helped us connect with users who came searching for the sale information on Twitter."

The exclusive flash sale on Twitter raised the maximum $50,000 in charitable donations for Stand Up To Cancer. It was also one of the top five sale days ever for the airline. Elevate, Virgin America's loyalty program, saw a 25% increase in sign-ups over the previous week.

"On Twitter, we had over four times the average follows and over two times the average mentions of @VirginAmerica during the campaign. We also had over 11,000 mentions of our hashtag. All of the engagement and conversations around our Promoted Trend and Promoted Tweets led to one of our most successful revenue generating days ever. More importantly, we were able to do it in a way that resonated with our guests and gave back to a great cause," explained a company spokesman when quizzed about the overall success of the campaign.

There are a couple of things well worth noting here. First, Virgin, as a group are very social media orientated and have had a social media mind even before online tools such as Twitter came along.

Second, they go into a lot of effort to monitor the success of their campaigns. They plan them carefully, link profit to social goodness and are careful not to overreach. For them the conversation is truly incremental.

## #2 GNC: Twitter helps GNC build a follower base for key selling season.

GNC wanted to quickly grow its follower base to be on par with its competitors in time for the summer, a key selling period for health and fitness retail.

To help achieve this GNC ran a highly targeted Promoted Account campaign for their @GNCLiveWell account and frequently optimized the campaign to maximize followers. GNC also enhanced their profile page with prominent branding that included additional promotion of the @GNCLiveWell handle.

The direct result of their actions was that GNC tripled the size of its follower base in only 15 days, allowing them to connect and engage with a broader audience around their summer marketing initiatives with timely coupons and in-store promotions.

## #3. Paramount Pictures: Twitter drives buzz and box office results for Paramount's *Super 8*.

Paramount's *Super 8*, a quirky film about an alien, a conspiracy and some school friends, which was hard to easily categorise, was challenged with a modest budget in a summer full of huge blockbusters. Their goal was simple: quickly increase awareness and ramp-up box office results for the opening weekend.

Paramount used a single Tweet combined with a Promoted Trend to exclusively announce early screenings a full day in advance of the premiere.

After igniting the conversation with early screenings, a second Promoted Trend ran the day of the film's premiere to keep the buzz and excitement high.

As a result of this exclusive, sneak-peak strategy, the Twitter exclusive sneak previews generated $1 million in box office receipts and because of the noise generated around it receipts for the opening weekend surpassed expectations by 52%.

## #4. National Parks Conservation Association (NPCA): National Parks Conservation Association @NPCA

National Parks Conservation Association (NPCA) leverages a current event to drive online actions.

The National Parks Conservation Association (NPCA) wanted to grow awareness of their cause as well as increase donations and petition signatures.

In order to get this done NPCA piggy-backed Promoted Tweets on an organically trending topic (#IfGovernmentShutsDown) to generate awareness of their fundraising and petitioning initiatives, as well as to encourage a call to action in support of their cause.

As a result over 5,200 people clicked on the link in the Tweet to contact members of Congress to support national park funding. The message was also picked up by Twitter's "Top Tweets" and was broadcast to an additional 1.1 million people. CNN broadcast the message as one of the most popular government shutdown Tweets. The extra publicity this provided generated a further income of fresh donations.

## #5. Venice Beach Suites & Hotel (Small Hotel) – Uses various social media channels to help deliver a very unique message

The owner of Venice Beach Suites & Hotel in LA, 62-year-old Andy Layman, spends a chunk of his day listening to the online chatter at Twitter and other social networking websites, hoping to join in.

Social media is an inexpensive way to find more of the type of traveller who already raves online about his eclectic, 25-room location. About three-quarters of the reviews on TripAdvisor, a major travel website, are positive, and this helps drive the conversation which converts into customers.

In the summer, Layman charges $130 to $305 a night for rooms, some of which have the building's original claw-foot bathtubs. Guests ride the 1939, birdcage-style elevator to the upper floors.

Engaging potential customers via social networking helps boost sales as well as manage expectations for the hotel. The latter is a crucial part of the hotel's social media strategy. Having its own specific period feel the Venice Beach Suites & Hotel cannot hope to compete with larger, slicker rivals unless the owner manages to engage the online population with a

conversation which clearly helps deliver the message
about the hotel's uniqueness.

The results so far have been encouraging with
sales growing by 10% towards the $1 million mark.
Against tough competition and increased operating
costs the manager/owner hopes to be able to strike just
the right note in each social media channel he is active
in, to help the hotel stand out.

### #6. Network Solutions: Use Twitter to Promote Larger-Than-Life Social Campaign

There is hardly anyone in the US (and many living
outside its borders) who have not heard of the Super
Bowl or know what it is. Similarly, there is hardly
anyone in the world who has not heard of GoDaddy.
Yet, Network Solutions a domain name registrar and a
hosting company was there before the latter and, in the
tech world, has had a history as illustrious as the
former.

Hurt by a media blitz by GoDaddy which upped
the stakes in risqué allusion and gave the hosting
company a reason to go viral, Network Solutions chose
the 2011 Super Bowl take a few well-aimed swipes at
their wealthier rival.

Unable to compete toe-to-toe with GoDaddy's
deep pockets and purchase of Super Bowl ad time the
company's ad agency decide instead to piggy back on
its ads, spoofing their content and looking to attract the
attention of media influencers and bloggers for the rest.

With a $200,000 budget, the company developed
a concept around Go Granny, "the original domain
girl," and created a series of mockumentary vignettes
featuring Academy Award-winner Cloris Leachman.

While the campaign was centered around one parody commercial hosted on YouTube, Twitter played a large role in the promotion and success of the campaign.

The social media director of the agency hired to oversee the job explained the concept in an interview for Ad Week magazine: "Go Granny's antics did not stop on YouTube. She took her sassy personality to drive traffic to the video. She took over Twitter for three one-hour long tweetcapades on the Friday, Saturday and Sunday of Super Bowl weekend. During the tweetcapades, @Go_Granny's tweets were carefully targeted to win the attention of influencers like Guy Kawasaki and Scott Monty, under the premise she was inviting people to her Super Bowl party. The team of powerful mommy bloggers at BlogHer participated in the tweetcapades as well, tapping into their extensive networks."

As a result of this approach, in five days, the campaign inspired more than 3,500 tweets and garnered nearly 20 million impressions across Twitter. On top of that, #GoGranny became a trending topic in Washington, D.C., and top influencers who tweeted about Go Granny included Gina Trapani and Brian Solis. Even more impressive, the company's sales of the .CO domain increased by more than 500% during Super Bowl weekend as a direct result of the campaign.

The valuable lesson learnt from this is that Twitter is an extremely helpful tool for generating buzz around an online social media campaign, but it needs support from other social outlets as well in order to reinforce the power of its reach.

Twitter is the closest thing we have to online TV in terms of passivity (YouTube which, technically, is like an online TV channel actually leads to high levels of interaction, while Twitter, according to the latest surveys is consumed passively by the bulk of its users).

The Network Solutions campaign was backed by blog posts and a Facebook campaign, alerting Facebook users to the Network Solution ads, emails were sent out to the customer base of the ad company, Network Solutions issued a press release and they also conducted a traditional media outreach campaign.

In addition there was a small team targeting blogs with high influence in specific circles, like women and mom bloggers, and these efforts were also coordinated with the Twitter campaign.

The Network Solution success on a budget many times smaller than their competitor's showed two important things: First, social media marketing works but not as a standalone channel, it is instead, an amplifier, increasing the influence, reach and impact of a small campaign which is, however, happening along traditional ad campaign channels. Second, there is no magic bullet. You cannot, for instance, hope to use YouTube, or Twitter and leave it at that. You need to coordinate everything so that everything feeds into itself in a truly, well-orchestrated media campaign.

**#7. How McDonald's, in Canada, used Twitter to increase its popularity.**
McDonald's is a difficult client. While the brand recognition is undeniable there is also the undeniably

well-recognised term 'McJob' and the fact that fast food has nutritional image issues, as a whole.

Although it used Twitter, essentially a global reach tool, to achieve that goal, what is notable here is the fact that they segmented the approach geo-targeting potential Twitter followers. Working through the Twitter account, @McD_Canada, the agency McDonald's hired had a budget of just $15,000 to work with. To achieve its aim and increase the online profile of McDonald's Canada, the agency used a variety of hashtags and Twitter keywords and a Twitter promoted account to become one of the 'suggested follow' choices on Twitter.

As a result, over the course of the campaign, McDonald's Canada gained 9,503 new followers. The campaign also drew in 14,200 profile views and resulted in a 4% overall engagement rate, which includes retweets, replies, favourites and clicks. This engagement rate is quite high when one considers that advertising click-through rates are generally sub-zero percentages.

The lesson learnt here is different to the one from Network Solutions we saw in the previous case study. The budget was substantially smaller and Twitter was used exclusively as the channel of the operation (which also narrowed down the metrics) but, just like the Network Solutions' campaign, this was a clearly thought-through, very precisely targeted effort. As a matter of fact the geotargeting of this campaign allowed it to become very specific to Canadian Twitter users which resulted in the high response rate.

The message here is that targeting is important. Both this campaign and the one in the case study before it used targeting in their efforts with differing degrees of precision. This is also reflected in the cost. Generally speaking, the less targeted your campaign is, the higher the outlay involved, becomes.

### #8. Nike uses Facebook to reach fans and build relationships.

When it comes to marketing and advertising Nike have practically written the rule book. The company has successfully turned a sports shoe business which has little to command it above other sports shoe companies into a lifestyle choice, where the brand is closely related to fans' feelings about particular sports, health, fitness and living.

It achieves this through TV ad campaigns, mostly, which have the kind of budget which can be confused for a telephone number. When Nike takes social media seriously, you know that it is not a thing which they have done lightly, in a "jump on the bandwagon" sort of way.

Case in point was their Facebook campaign. As Ricky Engelberg, Nike's Director of Sports, explained, the whole point was to do something that would "ignite the graph". The graph in question is Facebook's social graph and really, Nike was guided by a vision where a Father and son watching the Nike ad on TV would have a conversation where the son would say "I saw this already, on Facebook, and shared it with all my friends."

This is a tough target, to say the least, but it is exactly this kind of sweeping visions which allows Nike to become a leader in its field, by staking a very ambitious goal and then going for it.

To achieve this kind of eyeballs sharing on Facebook Nike took the unprecedented step of releasing its video ad on Facebook first, a couple of days before it was aired on Television. There is a video about the behind the scenes of the Facebook campaign on YouTube (Nike ads cost so much to make that even the making of them needs to be capitalised on) which can be watched through this URL: http://goo.gl/KO2ME.

The Nike Facebook campaign created the kind of buzz most companies would kill for and it also highlighted an important issue: If you really want to engage fans with a brand, you need to make them feel exclusive and special, rather than just part of the crowd you are marketing to.

This is true of social media which brings the personalisation of the web to a new level. It is this degree of personalisation which allows those who are part of the conversation in social media platforms to become engaged and actively take part in it.

## #9. Pringles, Coca Cola, Starbucks, Adidas and Red Bull do Facebook.

For the ninth case study I have taken the slightly unusual step of putting together a number of high-visibility brands in order to examine the similarity of their use of Facebook which makes them successful on that social media platform.

By choosing five I used certain criteria: I used brands which are representative of so called lifestyle products rather than essentials. I used brands which have large budgets because I did not want to become a limiting factor in what they could do. And I used brands which have stiff competition which means that success in social media marketing is a necessity in their marketing rather than a nice extra.

Facebook provides a limitation in itself in that the social media platform does not allow for a great deal of customisation. You may be a giant multi-national corporation or a mom-and-pop dime store, yet on Facebook you have the same capabilities in terms of what you can do in programming. In science limiting factors are revealing because they introduce the kind of artificial stress which leads to innovation. If we can all do the exact same things what makes us stand apart is the ingenuity we apply in how we do them.

With this in mind I examined the five brand pages on Facebook and the way they used the capabilities of the social media platform. What became apparent is that although the way each of the five big brands used its Facebook page was different, they all managed to create a strong following with extensive resharing of their content and an increase in the number of people who join the page, through strong engagement techniques which reinforced the emotional connection people feel with the brand through the use of games and competitions. They also increased engagement by creating innovative participation-inducing content that made it easy for those who followed the page (or those who came across it in their Facebook Wall) to become involved at a level that was comfortable to them.

What became immediately apparent is that big brands which succeed in social media are adept at employing two techniques whose social media marketing meaning we will look at next. Namely 'conversation' and 'telling a story'.

## 'Conversing' and 'Storytelling' two social media techniques which categorize the medium

When it comes to social media there are two terms which are constantly bandied about and these are 'telling a story' and 'having a conversation'.

Just like when it comes to the term 'social' most of us have some sort of understanding what these stand for and, just like in the term 'social' our understanding of what this means often leads to misunderstandings which then lead to social media marketing failures.

This is why this is a good opportunity to examine how these two terms apply to social media and how just how can they be successfully used.

Let's begin with the easier of the two which is the 'conversation'. If we assume that, until now, most online marketing was 'talking' at best, it stands to reason that talk went one way where you, the marketer, sent out a message and someone, the potential audience, listened.

In this tableau the effectiveness of your talking and its message was measured by how successful your bottom line was as a result of this. If you carried out no other forms of marketing then this talking (which happened through your website, online press releases, and online statements) became the principle means through which you communicated with your target audience.

Although this way works and there is a measuring mechanism in place which gauges its effectiveness, it works with the same haphazard, blind technique as traditional advertising. There is no true, personalisation, for instance. You talk about the same things to all. And there is no real way to see how those who hear what you say perceive your business or how much they love or hate what you do.

In social media conversation replaces talking and this changes everything in the way we communicate. The conversation which takes place through social media has to create the same subtlety and interest as a real, one-to-one conversation does. This requirement means that your subject matter, tone and even time of day of what you post are crucial to its success.

Here are the ingredients a social media conversation needs to have at its core:

> **Interesting topics to talk about** – this is not marketing and neither it is a carte blanche to bludgeon your audience with questions about "what they would like to see". You are the business, the brand, the social media presence. Find ways to have conversations which pique the interest of your audience and get them talking.

> **Personalisation** – This is a social media platform. Although you may have an audience of 100,000 plus you are still talking to each of them one at a time. Make sure you understand this and respond both in terms of sensitivity in what you post and how you then respond to those who respond to it.

> **Engagement** – You need to create engagement through social media in order to have a conversation. How you do it depends upon your skill in

responding to those who engage with your content and your ability to choose topics of conversation which are topical and of sufficient interest to elicit a response in the first place.

Provided you have these three ingredients in mind and work to make them happen in your social media content then you begin a process of true interactivity which will lead, in turn, to what social media marketers often blab about: the creation of brand ambassadors and word-of-mouth publicity. For either of these to happen, you need to leave those you converse with, with a positive experience of who you and what you do and a sense that you are different from your competition.

This takes, rather neatly, to the second requirement of successful social media marketing which is storytelling.

Essentially if you 'tell a story' in the totality of your social media marketing you achieve several things at once:

> Holistically, you begin to create content which in its totality achieves greater value than just the sum of its parts. This is an achievement and, as far as marketing is concerned, something which every brand strives for.

> You create interest. Those coming across a post, for instance, sense that there is much more to your business than just this and are more likely to seek out other content you have posted. This leads to

increased exposure, increased engagement and increased interaction – which should lead to increased business.

➢ You begin to differentiate yourself. Marketing is always about differentiation and social media marketing is all about differentiation. The moment you are seen as being different from everyone else you are also on your way to giving reasons to your target audience to do business with you rather than anyone else. This can only be achieved by you telling your unique 'story'.

Just how you integrate a conversation and telling a story in your social media communications is part of the challenge. Successful social media strategies are developed with a long-term view which tells a story, like parts of a puzzle and which, also, has sufficient flexibility to enable you to respond to topical issues as they arise.

If all this sounds like a tall order it is because it is. This is exactly why social media marketing is unsuccessful for many of the companies which engage in it. It is frequently seen as a new, untried, addition, which takes more and more of their time. Instead of allocating some time to think about it properly and decide how they will use it and what they will publicise, they do the knee-jerk response thing, which has them using social media as just another broadcast channel for their marketing messages.

It's bad, right? Use this to your advantage. Create a social media strategy and watch your company or brand get ahead of your competitors. More than that.

Create a real social media strategy and watch social media help you create a powerful online brand presence which really contributes to your bottom line profits.

## It's all about creating a clear signal

We live in a world that is getting noisier by the second. When you only have microseconds to catch someone's attention and hold it, and if in that action hangs your very survival you either get it very wrong, or very right.

In a recent trip to Greece I took my partner to see a local open air street market (called *La-eki*). These markets are a marvel of logistics in their own right. Hundreds of tiny stalls which offer everything from hand-made carpets to freshly laid eggs, fresh fruit and fish are set up overnight in tiny streets, closing them for the best part of the day and turning quiet backstreet neighbourhoods into colourful, noisy bazaars.

There is a long-standing tradition of such markets in Greece being set up on specific streets, on specific days of the week. They attract thousands of locals eager to take advantage of the low prices and they are part of the country's grey economy, creating jobs and providing a market for producers who might not otherwise be able to get their produce to the market any other way.

I like them for two reasons. First there is an amazing feeling of stepping back into the past when you walk through them. Suddenly, Google, the web, social networks and online marketing are about as useless and irrelevant as last week's fish catch. Second I can witness first-hand the harsh dynamics of Darwinism when it comes to marketing.

The stalls are packed closely together with many of the sellers, selling similar produce, frequently lumped together and having to vie with each other for the custom of a tightly packed throng which passes by.

In that setting there is little opportunity to stop and browse or window shop. There is a constant flow of people and most of these go up and down looking for the best prices or the freshest looking stuff to buy.

It is noisy. Stall holders yell their hearts out. They shout out prices, say something clever about their produce, make a comment about it being an unmissable opportunity. If you think there is a lot of 'noise' in online marketing, a single trip to a street market will convince you of the fact the of all the advantages the digital economy has to offer its civility and civilising way of conduct simply has to be the best.

Faced with such noise (and I have no idea how they manage to maintain their yelling from early morning to late afternoon, when the market is disbanded) sellers exercise both the crudest of traditional outbound marketing techniques: i.e. they simply yell the loudest and the longest and some of the most refined means of creating a signal I have ever seen.

To them, the throng passing by must seem like so many grey blobs, heads slightly down, holding non-descript plastic bags with produce or merchandise bought, looking at the stalls on either side of them (the market stalls are arranged on both sides of the street with a tiny path no more than a couple of metres wide left in the middle for people to come and go) and yet, their marketing success depends entirely upon their ability to connect with the individual.

This is one of the reasons I love the experience and, when I travel to Greece, I make a point of visiting such markets (there are cultural variations depending in which city you are in that I also find fascinating). Here, removed from the trappings of the web, immersed in a way of marketing which I fancy must have been active during the Ottoman Empire days over 400 years ago and might not be that much more different than Medieval stall markets over 1,000 years ago, you get to witness the ability to connect turned into a strength which leads to a sale.

For all their yelling, the most successful stall sellers are not the ones which simply yell the loudest but the ones which can pick you out of the crowd and address you personally and the ones which are clever enough to yell something which goes beyond a "Buy here. I have stuff to sell cheap" message.

To the consternation of my partner who, after a while, overloads and wants to go to a dark, quiet place and lie down for a while, I have spent long hours analysing how they do it, observing them first hand and, from my perspective, seeing the similarities with social media marketing.

Understand that street markets are cheap. There are many stalls selling similar produce. You can get, for instance, fresh tomatoes in stalls directly opposite each other and you can get fresh tomatoes in another dozen stalls up and down the street and adjoining side street. Prices, when in close proximity to each other, are the same. When they are separated by a couple hundred yards or more they are different but we are talking pennies. A difference small enough as to be negligible, even if you are penny-pinching.

So in a way, produce and merchandise there is commoditized. With price out of the way as a factor for choosing, and the display of the merchandise fairly uniform (there are simply not that many ways you can arrange fruit and vegetables on a metal trestle table) decisions come down upon such unfathomable variables as mood, where people end up (going after oranges I and my partner went up and down the street a few times looking at stalls. Having seen them all, we purchased from the one we then found to be nearest), and the seller's ability to catch their attention in the first place.

To achieve that street sellers employ two techniques which would not look out of place in a social media marketing situation. They broadcast (i.e. yell) a message which is distinctive enough to make some of the people in the throng slow down and take a second look, and then they personalise their marketing.

"Potatoes dug up yesterday," one stall holder I was watching in action yelled. Potatoes are cheap and to me they all look the same. They are not even very colourful and as this is a street market after all, what he was selling was all sorts of shapes and covered with the odd clod of dirt. None of the uniformly shaped, wax polished potatoes you see in a modern supermarket.

Vying with more colourful oranges, apples and mandarins all around him, he broadcast a message which seemed to hit home. Having potatoes which had just been dug up was obviously something which appealed as several women in the throng slowed down enough to actually take a look at the potatoes he was selling.

He then delivered his second master stroke of marketing: "Feed the entire family for a month," he said in a much quieter voice to a woman who had stopped and was looking at the potatoes.

"How much for two kilos?" she asked and he was in business.

For me, that man, at that moment, had been transformed into a marketing lion. He had refined a technique where what he broadcast to the masses was attractive enough to allow them to create a personalised image in their minds and then he marketed to each one he 'caught' this way, individually.

"Perfect potatoes for your princess," he said to me seeing that I had not moved for a few minutes and was standing there with my partner looking at his stall. The message made me smile and had I been a local, I would have bought some potatoes from him just for that.

It is this ability to create a clear signal amidst the noise that helps stall owners in noisy street markets survive and be successful and it is also this ability which needs to be developed in social media marketing.

Steve Jobs who, despite his flaws, had the selling instincts of a street market peddler, at his first staff meeting at Apple, after returning in 1997 told everyone present: "This is a very noisy world. So, we have to be very clear what we want them to know about us."

He was asking for focus of the message and the brand and a clear way to get that across. To engage the audience, much the same way, that potato seller in Greece managed to engage his clients.

It is no accident that Apple, in 2011, became the richest company in the world with a cash surplus which, at one point, exceeded that of the US government.

Social media marketing is new, in the ways, and the concepts we discuss such as 'brand ownership', creating 'brand ambassadors' for your products and 'creating a conversation', are new in the way we bandy them about. But nothing is really new under the sun. As my example with the Greek street market so colourfully illustrated these are practices which any thriving market needs in order to produce successful businesses within it, and apparently, every thriving market has already had in one form or another.

When a street stall seller manages it armed with nothing else than a good larynx and the need to feed his family, it is impossible for us to not be able to find ways to do it online, with all the tools at our disposal. Nor is size a barrier, as two social media marketing success stories clearly illustrate.

## Two exceptional social media presences

As 2011 was winding down and the final edits, changes and additions to this book were being made the web appeared to be in the grip of one social media PR meltdown after another.

With just weeks to go before Christmas, PayPal was rushing to throw its hat into the ring with the very public mishandling of a case regarding a humorous blog called Regretsy and a Christmas donation drive for poor children being organized through its pages.

The particulars of this PR meltdown apart what makes this interesting, beyond the fact that it happened

118

at Christmas and a PayPal representative went on record saying that it was OK to donate money to sick cats as a worthy cause, according to PayPal guidelines, but not to poor people, is that it followed the exact same pattern of all other social media PR meltdowns.

There was the same incredible faceless corporation approach to a customer service problem. The situation was not addressed, when it was addressed corporate speak came into play, when the inevitable social media meltdown happened there was the usual ill-judged response (PayPal even tried to delete negative messages accumulating at a fantastic rate on its Facebook page) and when the inevitable back tracking and corporate apology came, the word 'sorry' was off the list.

All this only makes those companies which get social media, right now, that more exceptional. One of them is Ford.

Ford's social media success comes down to one man: Scott Monty. Scott has been active in social media for some time. He is good at understanding the nuanced approach required and he totally gets how to turn social media engagement into corporate public relations gold.

Scott is down-to-earth, super busy and yet quick to respond to social media questions, answers and even posts, and has an engaging personal style which he has translated into a corporate social media approach that works for Ford.

Scott Monty became Head of Social Media at Ford in 2008 and he was quick to put in a Social Media strategy which included the entire company. The first thing he did was create multiple Social Media channels on:

> ➤ Facebook
> ➤ Twitter
> ➤ YouTube
> ➤ Flickr
> ➤ Google+

More than that, he created a campaign designed to humanize Ford so that it went from being a giant car manufacturer to being a company staffed by people who were passionate about the cars they made and who connected with and talked to potential car buyers and Ford enthusiasts about those cars.

This turned traditional marketing principles, which keep the company buttoned down and working from a single message which comes from the very top, on its head.

Within a year of Ford's campaign being implemented the results were tangible:

> ➤ 11 million Social Networking impressions
> ➤ 5 million engagements on social networks (people sharing and receiving)
> ➤ 11,000 videos posted
> ➤ 15,000 tweets.. not including retweets
> ➤ 13,000 photos
> ➤ 50,000 hand raisers who had seen the product in person or on a video and who said that they want to know more about it when it comes out and 97% of those don't currently drive a Ford vehicle.
> ➤ 38% awareness by Generation Y about the product, without spending a dollar on traditional advertising ( Fords model "Fusion"

doesn't have that awareness after two years of being out in production and yet it has received hundreds of millions of dollars in traditional marketing spend).

How did Scott do it? The paradox of social media is that it is not a secret. Scott himself makes no secret of the social media marketing strategy he created for the company and actually there is a presentation he has created called *Zero to 60: Ford's Social Media Story* which can be seen online here: http://goo.gl/O8N06

What becomes obvious, looking at it, is how good Scott Monty is at getting the people at Ford to actually put their passion for their work on the web.

It is also evident that the reason Ford is so exceptionally successful at using social media is because the right social media marketer has met the right CEO. Alan Mulally, Ford's CEO, loves cars, loves his company and loves getting his passion across to the public.

Like most CEOs of that ilk he is the kind of guy whom, had you met him in a pub, he would have converted you into a loyal fan of his company by the end of the evening. In managing Ford, Alan focuses on doing what he does and leaves the social media handling in the hands of Scott, whom he actually listens to.

At corporate level this kind of relationship between a company CEO and a social media marketer is so rare as to be truly exceptional. As exceptional, as a matter of fact, as Ford's success, which totally concedes the point.

One example of Scott Monty's way of working in social media and its effectiveness is generating customer loyalty (almost a dead concept in the 21st century) and sales from word-of-mouth online publicity.

Scott said that his "Jewel in the Crown" is the Ford Fiesta Movement (the URL of which can be accessed athttp://fiestamovement.com) that involved selecting 100 socially vibrant individuals who were provided with the European version of the Ford Fiesta 18 months prior to it being manufactured and released in the USA. These socially media aware fanatics were then encouraged to share their experience with the Ford Fiesta over a six month period on their Blogs, Twitter, Facebook, Flickr and YouTube channels, generating more publicity and buyer-generating interaction than any amount of top-down advertising would have been hard-pressed to even match, let alone beat.

The beauty of it is that the cost itself, when compared to traditional advertising, was negligible.

Ford's social media success can be boiled down to seven, relatively simple, points we can look at in order to think how they can be applied to any other type of business.

> Consumers trust corporations less and less. The rise of social media allows corporations to be more transparent (Scott Monty's creed at Ford) and allow other people through word of mouth to create trust for you through Social Media (it amplifies your message).
> Social media allows us to communicate. Reach out to those who are listening and let them do the talking for you and

connect with people like themselves, helping to propagate the values of your brand.

➢ Be real. Let those you connect with understand that you are real people just like them and are passionate about what you do. Scott Monty has regular sessions with Ford's CEO, Alan Mullaly, where they simply answer questions put directly to Alan through Twitter.

➢ Create a buzz which can get people involved. Run a competition involving Social Media, just like the 100 giveaway Fiesta Movement which required people to actually apply and tell Ford why they would be suitable candidates to receive to drive a Ford Fiesta for six months. The power of this, when handled correctly, can be seen in Michelle McCormack's YouTube video application: http://goo.gl/LbjJq.

➢ Aggregate your content for maximum impact. In Ford's case they created the website http://fordfiestamovement.com where they crowd-sourced content which they never edited (it did wonders for their sense of authenticity and credibility).

➢ Implement more than one social media channel. Reach out to as many people as possible through as many different platforms in order to generate a sense of buzz, where they meet your activities and company name, wherever they turn.

> The last point is the most crucial of all however. "Get On Board" the executive team and the board of directors. Without them you end up fighting a losing battle where the social media marketer has to convince his own people of the effectiveness of what he proposes to do, every step of the way. That's an approach which never works. Social media requires speed of execution, flexible thinking and more trust than any company, of any size, has ever been able to put in anyone and anything in the past. And this is the challenge to solve when it comes to creating a corporate social media presence that actually works the way it should.

To understand the power social media has in marketing but also in guiding the development of products consider the concept car Evos, unveiled by Ford at the Frankfurt Auto show in September 2011. Apart from the expected sleek lines, gull-wing doors and futuristic styling the car is designed to be socially networked. Always connected to the cloud, which allows it to know the driver's work schedule, constantly keep tabs on traffic and weather conditions, and assist and monitor the driver in an attempt to enable a seamless lifestyle between home, office and car, all linked by access to the driver's personal information.

Ford wanted to create a vehicle which, according to their literature, gives its driver the ability to tap into this "personal cloud" of information at any time, for example, picking up where the driver left off on that favourite song they were listening to inside the house. The vehicle's smart systems monitor its driver's "physical state and workload," adjusts the car's handling, heating, cooling and music to suit the driver's level of alertness, perhaps even keeping him from falling asleep. The aim with the Evos is that Ford will have a "...car that gets to know you and can act as a personal assistant to handle some of the usual routines of a daily commute."

This kind of thinking, where the car is also capable of tapping into its owner's social network and updating its location, blurs the lines of offline and online in social media networking and simply makes 'social' something we do with all the tools at our disposal, everywhere, all the time.

We started this section with the intention to look at two exceptional social media cases. Ford, has been lucky with Scott Monty and the trust its CEO puts in him. The other social media success story has simply been lucky with its CEO and it is none other than Virgin, and Richard Branson.

Those who have met Richard know him as a guy who is little brash, very straight talking and has a highly developed sense of mischief coupled to a cut throat competitive drive.

Forced to be the underdog for most of his life, destined to challenge the status quo with meagre resources he developed, perhaps, out of necessity a social media approach to doing business.

Starting entrepreneurship at a time in Britain when 'the old boy network' was very much in effect, he was forced to employ social media tactics instinctively in order to capture the attention of the public.

Famous, amongst them perhaps was his 1980s stunt of dressing up as a pirate and boarding a British Airways plane where he then had to be forcibly removed from. The move was designed to draw attention to the fact that British Airways, a Virgin Air rival who was enjoying better gates and better treatment at Heathrow, was overcharging its passengers, essentially robbing them blind, and offering a low-quality service in return.

The stunt made the nine o'clock news in all major BBC channels in the UK, gaining more exposure for the Virgin brand than any amount of advertising could have got it, and creating a social media buzz around it and what it stood for (better prices and better service).

We are used to social media standing as a shorthand for something very specific: online network platforms usually such as Facebook, Google+, Twitter and YouTube. We forget that social media has been around in low-tech formats since the beginning of time. Graffiti carved on aqueduct walls across the Roman empire extoling the virtues of a local Centurion or drawing attention to the failings of a particular house of ill repute, is social media.

Opinions offered on consumer products, around a cup of tea and biscuits after a Church service is social media. The sponsoring of motor events and classical music concerts by Banks and oil companies, is social media.

126

From the point of view of those who share the opinion, the review, the product, the idea, the intention is to actually recommend something based on their own experience or to condemn it, based on the same.

For companies and brands (and even our local Centurion in a lonely Roman outpost town) the intention is to improve their image, to create empathy and connection with their public and to enjoy a much better relationship with it than might otherwise have been possible.

While this sounds Machiavellian in approach it is anything but. Our lonely Centurion could employ Rome's well-rehearsed PR machine with the marching of troops, brandishing of insignia and the expenditure of coin but that would be expensive and may not really get the message across. It could also backfire in a reactive manner, unsettling the populace and leading to more trouble.

He would probably find it much easier to be kind to a couple of well-known, local graffiti artists who could then be trusted to practise their art and spread the word about his kindness, humanity and compassion.

In the process the Centurion himself finds that he is changing. He exercises acts of human kindness as part of his duty, rather than mercilessly laying down Roman Law, backed by the might of the local Legion's spears and swords.

He takes an interest in local affairs and, when he has erred, or has passed an unpopular judgement, he goes to great lengths to explain his action to the public he rules over so that they better understand the pressure he works under and the particulars of each circumstance.

As he understands them more and more he finds that he can do his job better and make fewer unpopular decisions which are not truly warranted. The public, in return, is quick to maintain law and order and praise him where they can, wary of losing him and having him replaced by some other, harsher Centurion.

Everyone wins.

While my example here is exaggerated out of necessity and viewed through the selective prism of business marketing, it should not surprise us to discover moments in history from Alexander the Great (a leader famous for his common touch) to Bill Clinton's famously populist approach which employ exactly this kind of thinking, sometimes instinctively, sometimes by design and, more often than not, as a combination of the two.

What is common to all those moments is the fierce loyalty and pathos they engender. Alexander's army followed him to the ends of the Earth and his subjects were willing to make him a god. Bill Clinton enjoys a popularity which far outweighs the achievements of his presidency and which is due to the perception that people 'know' him.

## What lessons can be learnt for businesses in social media marketing?

We are very fond, these days, of using the word 'lessons' for everything. Lessons are learnt in politics, trading, eCommerce, the web, investment banking and finance and social media marketing is no exception.

'Lessons' however implies some kind of traditional learning where we open up the dusty tomes

128

containing the knowledge of the past and social media marketing is a 21st century concept for which there is no adequate past.

The beauty of it, what creates the opportunities and allows us to envision a world refashioned to work better and cause fewer problems, lies in the fact that we now get to make the rules up as we go along.

There is a fallacy here which I need to explain first. We believe, in any sphere of learning, that there are somehow rules which are created and which once created must be obeyed. We extend this erroneous belief to social media marketing. If we extend the fallacy to its logically natural conclusion we can then say that now's the time to create some rules which everyone else who comes late to the party will have to follow.

The argument sounds as ridiculous as it is. Rules in any activity are born out of sound logic which dictates the principles of the dynamics which govern that activity.

When you throw a ball in the air you enter into a contract, of sorts, with the planet whereby how far you can throw a ball to another person is governed by the mass of the ball, the mass of the planet, the angle of the ball's trajectory and the amount of energy you pour into the act of throwing. There are rules which govern all this, but they cannot be 'created' nor can they be changed. They need, instead, to be discovered.

It is the same with social media marketing. Although it is a brand new form of activity on the web and we are in the process of finding out what works and what doesn't the rules really need to be discovered more than made up. Discovery, unfortunately, requires pain.

We learn what works and what doesn't, invariably, through failure.

Luckily, in the short time that social media marketing has been going on, we have managed to clock up a number of high profile failures which, when examined, allow us to create a road map to better social media marketing techniques by examining the assumptions which have not worked as well as we expected.

## Six myths about social media marketing you need to be aware of

In my travels across Europe, Russia and, a little less frequently these days, the US, I invariably come across practices, opinions and beliefs regarding the use of social media marketing which fall into one my six social media marketing myths list.

▸ **Social media is about the "media."** In other words, many companies look at Facebook, Twitter and other networks as a new mass broadcast mechanism which is easier and cheaper to use than their more traditional channels. Their social media strategy amounts to little more than creating a presence on Twitter and Google+ and having a Facebook fan page. Twitter messages are little more than 'lifts' taken from their marketing literature, Facebook messages are calls to buy or check out an offer on their website. They do not understand that social media is more about 'social' than media. Just as you would not take too kindly to a travelling salesman coming into your favourite bar and starting to shout out his offers, so there has to be learnt some respect regarding the social medium being used. The tone and content used have to be adjusted to fit in with the audience expectations which then, if used correctly, would automatically determine what is posted in each social media network, and how, so that it becomes more likely to work there.

The limitations of each medium are governed both by the perceived demographic and the limitation of the format itself. Twitter, for example, only allows you 140 characters of content. Facebook, recently lifted its posting limited to over 60,000 characters but it still requires an attractive picture to help a comment stand out in the stream and generate a response. Google+ is excellent when it comes to eliciting more in-depth replies and engagement and it allows you the kind of formatting you could put in a blog post but you do need a heading and a subject which is likely to catch the attention of an audience which is, at this point in time at least, more likely to think deeply about what you have posted and comment on it, at some length.

The point is that unless you understand the medium, what it does and how it is used by its members you are unlikely to post anything which works, in any social media marketing channel. Social network members these days are easy to annoy by what they perceive as spam, they will either report your posts, block your profile or simply ignore you. If any of these occurs, you will most likely end up wasting time and money and will probably come to the conclusion that "social media marketing is not working for me".

▸ **Control is possible.** Companies are hidebound by tradition and the old ways of doing things. This seeps down from business training and many of those who graduate from business schools, today, somehow end up spouting the mantra of "our company profile is sacred. We need to have complete control of our company image." For me those who say that, and believe it, miss the point completely. Yes a company's image is crucial but a company is never created to have an image. The image it has and the reputation it builds up are the direct result of the way it carries out its business and the way it communicates with its customers and to think otherwise is to forget what business is all about. Similarly, communication, in my book, is not about memos, advertising campaigns or slogans. Communication is something which takes place at every level of a business and at every opportunity this business has, to communicate. This is from the way emails are sent out to the way a product or service is delivered and the way the company's reps follow up with the aftersales service.

Communication is everything because it establishes the tone, voice and personality of the company and it becomes instrumental in the opinion those who receive those communications then form about it. If you think you are going to shape that opinion based on a few Tweets, some Facebook messages and a couple of posts on Google+ you are deeply mistaken.

To succeed in social media you need to follow that overtired, overused and overrated phrase: "Build it and they will come" and here, when paraphrased to "do what you do, better than anyone and your reputation and company image will take care of itself" it really works.

‣ **Social media is a distinct channel.** Frequently I have been called in to 'fix' social media campaigns which bear no connection to anything else the company is doing. Tweets, for instance, go online without anyone bothering to keep the Twitter team up to date on company offers or company developments or company problems (and we saw in Chapter 4 how the Blackberry Twitter team was Tweeting away while the company's reputation, unbeknown to them, was undergoing a public meltdown). Social media is new and needs even deeper integration with the company and its services than any other kind of marketing. Much of this has to do with the need for speed in both broadcasting a message and responding to online developments. In the past it might have been 'OK', for instance, to let the team handling the newspaper ads know about a development when it was either over or at a much later stage. Newspaper ads are fixed in their message and have a one-way broadcast capacity which perfectly justifies this approach of handling the flow of information within the company. This clearly is not going to work when Tweets can go around the globe within a half hour and a company can find itself becoming the trending topic on the basis of its lack of information (i.e. Blackberry) or its inability to respond (i.e Unilever with its Ragu PR disaster).

Speed changes everything and the companies which fail to understand this and then factor it into the way they work, frequently find social media hard to handle. A nine-to-five, five day a week, kind of system of communication, at the time when the internet never sleeps is unjustified. So is a system of internal communications where a Tweet has to go to a manager who has to get authorisation from his line manager who needs to be confident that the company's chairman is not going to disapprove, before it is published. Trust is the currency by which social media marketing runs. There has to be trust within the company that everyone understands how to use social media marketing and there has to be trust outside the company when it comes to communicating with its customers and those customers communicating with their own contacts and so on. Will mistakes never happen? Well, even within the perfect communication format, when the company messages come out pitch-perfect and with the regularity of clockwork, there will be problems. It is quite possible that a perfectly timed and pitched Tweet finds someone at the wrong moment, short of sleep and with an axe to grind. What is really important is that the company has the ability to respond so that it can manage what is going on in social media. A Tweet gone wrong may ruffle some PR feathers but it's not a disaster. A company which is incapable of responding and either ignores what is going on, hoping the noise will go away (Blackberry and Unilever have both been guilty of such behaviour) or deletes Tweets and Facebook messages which are negative (PayPal during its very public showdown with humorous blog, Egretsy, did just that) then becomes the story itself, fuelling the fire and drawing even more attention.

‣ **Companies should build their own social network**. Somehow, the words 'social network' appear to have become the Holy Grail of marketing for many companies. I have had CEOs explain to me how their companies' products were perfectly suited for social media marketing because they created a social subset of people and all the company now needed to do was create a social network which all these people which bought the products or services of the company would instantly join, become great friends, share content centred around the company's products, exchange stories about how great these products were and how they were simply dying to give up their online time on an unpaid basis and become fanatical brand ambassadors. After listening to the serious proposal of how great it would be for the company to own its own social network which would become the hub for recruiting the untold millions of potential customers who yet did not know what was good for them, my stock reply is always along the lines of the chances of cats and dogs lying down together, the heavens opening up and Apocalypse occurring before that mortgage loan I took out gets called in. In plain speak this is a pipe dream which makes perfect sense when presented on the whiteboard in the corporate conference room but which has nothing to do with reality.

Apple has, arguably, one of the most iconic brands on the planet with hundreds of thousands of fanatical Apple product buyers and, yes, even unpaid brand ambassadors who actually spend a lot of time sermonizing about Apple products in social networks. Does Apple have a social network? No. Would it like to? Most probably, but it also has the sense to understand that a social network is something which is incredibly difficult to build and almost impossibly difficult to do well and since there are established, accepted social networks out there like Twitter, Facebook and Google+ to actually go and build a new one is an exercise in flawed thinking, rather than good business sense.

‣ **Social media provides cheap crowd-sourcing.** Companies hope that the massive pull of numbers in a social media environment will somehow allow them to create a massive, accurate, unpaid and willing market research base. I understand that on the face of it there is a certain amount of logic here which goes along the lines of if you ask ten people down the street what they would like to taste in a beer and you get eight of them mentioning something specific and then you go out and make it you are onto a winner everyone will love. When it comes to social media (and even people down the street) the approach is flawed and riddled with variables you cannot adequately take into account.

Social media can provide many things but using your social media marketing to do cheap research upon which you can then base company decisions is akin to running a straw poll in prison about fashion. The chances that you will get a winning answer you can use are so infinitesimally small as to make the idea sound crazy. If there are experts on your company products they should be within your own company working for you.

‣ **Social media can lead to sales**. This is the part which when I debunk I can often see in the CEOs' eyes the thought emerging on why they should even hire me. The thought that social media is just another sales channel and all you need is someone to tell you 'how' to use it correctly so you can then put it in effect and make sales come flowing in, is one of the most commonly held myths I encounter.

The funny thing is that social media, when handled correctly, can lead to sales but for that to happen the social network you use to communicate has to be established as a channel through which information flows bi-directionally. It then becomes a channel which creates engagement and conversation and establishes trust and then, and only then,  does it allow for limited-time offers or special deals to flow through an already established network audience which can then be leveraged to maximise sales of a particular product at a particular time. The "Fragile: Handle With Care!" label should come as standard with every social media network a company intends to use. The danger here is much worse because the moment you 'break' the way you use a social network it does not stop working, rather it backfires with spectacularly negative results.

## So what can be done?

We looked at my list of the six social media myths which govern corporate usage of social media precisely so we can see how easy it is to fall into the trap of thinking that nothing has changed, that going digital is just the same as being traditional only with lower costs and greater reach.

To understand the depth of this fallacy I often recount a time in Australia when I was 13. I worked as a paperboy. The neighbourhoods, where I lived, were sprawling and the distances were huge and my job was to ride in the back of a mini moke (a type of open top Jeep) and throw a tightly rolled up newspaper into a yard as the driver went by (making it, I guess a kind of drive-by). He would blow once on a whistle to let the house owner know his paper had just been delivered.

Now, suppose, instead of a rolled up newspaper to throw I had an eight kilogram slab of marble. Great surface for carving news upon, used to great effect by the ancient Greeks. Elegant, cheap (if you have a local marble quarry handy) and durable adding great value to what was inscribed upon it, which is why it was so popular, I guess, in ancient Greece. Would I then be able to hold down the job I did? Would it be even feasible? I am not even sure the mini moke could handle the weight of all those tablets to begin with.

The length of time separating ancient Greece and its favourite medium of inscription and my paperboy job in Australia helps illustrate how a change of medium has the ability to change everything.

Had the mini moke and the paper round been around at the time when people inscribed on marble tablets my bet is that the paper round would have been organised differently. While the medium is never the message its limitations and strengths change everything, every time.

With that thought in mind let's go and see just what social media marketing allows you to do which you cannot do using any other kind of marketing (or at least do either as well or as cost-effectively – charges which can be successfully levelled at the marble tablet paper round job).

## Six steps to social media success

Balance works in everything, from nature and mathematics to physics and social sciences. Just as there are six myths which those who implement social media incorrectly frequently buy into, so there are six steps which can help social media marketing work the way it is supposed to.

The very last thing I want to do right here is be prescriptive. Prescriptions are always rigid, by default, and allow little leeway for truly transformative experiences to take place. Social media is a transformative channel in every sense of the word and social media marketing has the potential to completely change the way a company is perceived by those who may need its products or services.

We saw this with Ford, in a very positive way and we saw the impact a failure can have with both Netflix and Blackberry. Because social media is primarily about being social and everything else becomes secondary, there are specific steps which can be taken to make sure that 'social' remains at the forefront of online activities.

▸ **Make sure social marketing is in real time.** Social media marketing provides an instant channel of communication for customers. This then also means that it becomes an easy way for them to vent their frustration when things do not go according to plan (from their perspective). Not only must you, as a marketer, have real-time communication in place which informs everyone on time, about everything of value to them, but you must also closely monitor responses and have a coherent, actionable plan in place for a situation in which something now appears to be wrong. If you do not have a means of tackling this the moment it becomes an issue, hiding behind corporate announcements which are scheduled to happen at an appointed hour is not going to fix anything nor is ignoring the problem and hoping it will go away, going to work.

▸ **Internal communications are crucial.** If you want your social marketing to be part of your corporate outreach program you'd better make sure that those responsible for it are kept in the loop and know when things are wrong before anyone else. If you fail in this you are turning your employees into lambs sent to the slaughter. They can very quickly become demoralized, frustrated and suddenly in doubt of the very company they work for, this will inevitably show in the style of communication as well as their social media response times.

‣ **Social media marketing is about communication.** You have a social media marketing campaign in place so you can communicate with those who know about your company and what it does and those who you hope will want to find out. Even if you have not taken on-board the first point about social media marketing being carried out in near real-time and even if you are so corporate-mentality bound that you cannot envision the possibility that international customers of your products might not want to stick to your time zone, you still need to have a plan on how to really communicate with those you reach through social media, addressing issues and concerns that affect your products.

‣ **Say you're sorry.** It sounds silly but an apology when things go wrong works wonders. The time of the faceless corporation is so last century and today it only serves to annoy those you want to keep as customers against stiff competition. We all know that whenever a corporate façade is presented either things are really wrong and no one is admitting culpability or no one really cares – or both. Stick to outmoded models of communication and you are really missing the whole point of social media marketing and personalization.

‣ **Give timelines.** Is there a problem? Acknowledge it and say when it's going to be resolved. Even if the timeline is approximate, communicating provides evidence that someone cares and is doing something to fix the issue. Similarly if you have announced a new product launch and are stoking up the steam you'd better have a timeline to present to everyone. Vagueness, online, only prevents everyone from taking you seriously.

> **Understand what you are doing.** Social media marketing is about letting go of rigid control and beginning a real dialogue whereby your customers get to know who you really are and how passionate you are about the products you are selling. That is your only hope of actually converting eyeballs, shares, 'Likes' and impressions into the kind of brand awareness that leads to sales. To capitalize on this you need to rekindle your own passion for business (if you have started to go stale) or grasp what you need to do in order to successfully transmit this to the social media public.

## Social media and business

In the short time social media has been available as a means of promoting and communication the social media marketing landscape has been littered with the corpses of failed social media campaigns and failing social media marketing initiatives from some of the biggest names in the corporate marketing field.

The truth is that much of what is required to succeed in social media goes against the grain of much of the traditional wisdom of businesses and corporations. Transparency, as a rule, was regarded as being an enemy to image-management, veracity and authenticity in marketing were anathema to professional marketers, real-time communication and the need to respond to complaints from customers, even when those complaints have a greater foundation in fantasy than reality, has traditionally been regarded as counter-productive and undesirable.

Here's the thing though. We live in a time where there is more noise than signal in marketing. The commoditization of almost everything has made it next to impossible to differentiate a service or a product from its competitors and the ever shrinking attention span of the online population is making it harder for companies and their marketing departments to grab and hold the attention of those they need to market to.

This often leads to knee-jerk reactions, bandwagon jumping and the adoption of fads and trends (like give-aways on Facebook) as if they are the 'silver bullet' needed to do the job. The truth is both simpler and more difficult than most people think.

Let's start from the simple things first. Social media has taken us into a brand new direction from which will have to emerge new ways to market and new ways to do business and new ways to get information and pretty much, new ways to do almost anything which involves human interaction.

Five years from now this will be so ingrained in the online population modus operandi and so integrated in the DNA of every company that there will no longer be a 'social media' to use as a marketing channel. There will be just marketing and we will all be doing it.

The challenge which social media marketing presents us with is that of the company, the corporation or even the individual working from home, having to engage with a massive audience on a one-to-one basis. Obviously this cannot be achieved.

Yet, that is exactly what is required and the web makes it possible. Businesses, in the last century, were fond of marketing campaigns which contained slogans to the effect of "serving every customer, one customer at a time" – each business, back then, found its own way to get this across in its promotion, but they all, more or less, used it. Back then was as universal in marketing as it was meaningless. It was meant to create the image of personalisation in an audience which was being marketed to in anything but a personalized manner.

Billboards, television, radio and newspapers were employed as the channels used to, paradoxically, get the personalized message to the masses, in a mass-communication, faceless way. At the time, because we did not know any better and because those means of communication were all there was, companies thought that by using personalized slogans they were 'getting the job done' so to speak, in telling their potential customers that they provided a personal service.

Today, social media marketing works exactly in the personalized manner those ads of the past were supposed to make us think company marketing worked.

A single blogger with an axe to grind and an engaging way of expressing themselves is quite capable of producing so much bad publicity for a company as to ruin its reputation, provided, of course, the company does nothing to counter it.

Whenever I bring this up in presentations those who are in denial over the benefits of social media point out the wastefulness of such actions and how resources which could better be used in providing customer service (why, do they always bring up customer service?) are now diverted towards damage control.

143

The counter-argument is that this is a dialogue and not damaging per se. Even a powerful complaint which has a valid basis and can be backed up by solid data can be turned into an opportunity to cast positive light on a company if it is handled correctly.

I will use here an example from my own experience with Blackberry. Had the RIM co-CEO and founder of the company, Mike Lazaridis, appeared the moment the Blackberry service failed and told the world how vital Blackberry was for business (implicit message No 1) and how he felt like his right arm had just been hacked off with a machete (implicit message No 2) and how it would all be up and running in x number of days and that he was truly, madly, sorry about the outage, he would have succeeded, arguably, in raising the company's profile, creating sympathy for the brand and generating a buzz around it all which might have, perversely, led to more sales and drawn attention to some of unique selling point of Blackberry (its secure email and messaging communication) which is lost when compared to its feature and app-rich competitors.

He didn't.

Instead, four days after the outage had started he made a lacklustre appearance on a company video where he said "sorry, we've let you all down" – his company now faces a lawsuit from users in the US and Canada asking for compensation and RIM's stock is in free-fall, with a third quarter posting of a loss close to half a billion dollars.

The point is that social media is the worst possible channel to use for traditional corporate marketing and traditional company responses.

We live in a time where our patience, as individuals, with corporate facelessness and corporate sound bites is remarkably thin. We have all had experiences of the malfeasance of corporations driven by questionable motives and short-sighted perceptions of the company/client interaction. We have all had it with non-accountability in government, banking institutions and the companies we buy products from. What we now want is to matter. We all want to be taken seriously when we want to. We want to be able to cut through what can charitably call bovine manure and get to the real heart of things. Social media all about this real, no-frills connection which allows us to assess a brand and a company directly and have them make us feel that our assessment matters.

Given this fact you will ask, OK, suppose I am game. I can take my global mega-corp and turn it into a social media darling, what do I need to do to make sure that my social media marketing works for me rather than against me?

Surprisingly, again, the answer is simple:

‣ **Be Real** – give your company a unified voice and tone for talking to the outside world and make sure that this is informed, internally, by everything your company does.

‣ **Be engaging** – my guess is you did not go into business because you wanted to be bored to death. So, why is your social media marketing about products, services, specifications and prices? Which would you respond to best? A legal firm which gave you and endless list of litigations they won and the case number marking the legal precedent each set or a simple: "We won't go home until we get you off," promise which is backed by the premise that "we are divorced and have no life, but we are married to our work."

Faced with an endless list of potential candidates who present me with their successes I know which one I would go for. Find the fire which made you go into business and turn it into a vision you can communicate in a few simple sentences.

› **Be responsive** – Has someone said something great about your company? Thank them and share it with the world. Has someone said something negative? Respond to them, seek to understand what went wrong and if they are right tell everyone what lessons have been learnt.

This kind of approach requires a fundamental change from the old competitive mentality which saw each customer as a hard-fought acquisition and each competitor as a competitor to a cooperative model where your customers and you really want the same thing: a great experience in the transaction you are putting in place and the ability to answer a real need.

How you crack this exactly depends upon what fires you up and how you then translate it into social media interaction in order to really do something meaningful. Fail to grasp this and, well... we already have seen the alternatives on offer.

## How to Make Sure you 'Get It'

When I worked in national newspapers in the UK, in our downtime, in the newsroom, we had a small bet going. We scoured the local press (a valuable source of leads at times) and bet which local paper would ask the most number of times, in the year, their readers to tell them what they wanted to see in the newspaper.

I will tell you immediately why this is wrong but before I do let's start with why it's done.

When you see a "what would you like to see here?" call you can bet your last buck that the editor is pressed for time, has failed to generate enough local content in the newspaper, is uncertain of the target audience, has failed to generate engagement with the paper (local papers need a certain amount of engagement in order to feel that they fulfil their role as community newspapers) and he is uncertain of what the newspaper is really there to do and which direction he should head towards.

He is also labouring under the entirely misguided feeling that by having a call like that in his newspaper he is making it more open, interactive and engaging (something along the lines of "it is your paper written for you) and he is, subconsciously, shifting the balance of the blame for the success of its content from himself and his team to the newspaper's readers.

When you run a newspaper, whether it is a national behemoth or a local community servicing a few hundred souls, you are there to do a job. Your job is to generate news which touch the core of your readership's interests and which reflect their personality, community and passions. It is no different in social media. When you create a social media presence you are not there to just put up what you want because it happens to be what your organisation does or where your interests lie. Your job is to really find, amongst the potential millions who may see what you post, that subset which will be

touched by what you post, represented by its content
and engaged by it.

It really is that simple.

When Google opened the doors of Google+ to
brands, I lost count of the number of times I saw Brand
Pages start with a "Here we are, what would you like to
see here?" message (for the record, *Times* magazine did
it, *The Guardian* did it and even *Mashable* did it). The
same message was posted by NASA, NPR, the Al
Jazeera English, Fox8 News, PBS, NBC, *The Independent*,
as a matter of fact irrespective of whether you were a
news gathering service (like most of the culprits
mentioned), an aerospace agency or a social media blog
(like *Mashable* which was born on the web *for* the web)
the norm suddenly seemed to be to call upon a potential
audience they did not even know they had to tell them
what they wanted to see (even the *Huffington Post*
became an offender with its Politics section asking the
same question).

I will not even go into the obvious fact that when
you ask an audience you are unsure of what they would
like to see the danger is that you will actually get a
response. Suppose, for instance, the question fell upon
the attention of a devoted Search for Extra-Terrestrial
Intelligence (SETI) group? Would NASA really have
spent the rest of its online time discussing ETs on its
Google+ pages?

What this crass approach to crowdsourcing
demonstrates is the ease with which a new medium
(like social media) or a new platform (like Google+) can
rob even seasoned news executives who should know
better of their sense of what they are there to do and
how to do it.

You are on the web. You are using a social media platform and you are in control of your content. This puts you in the hot seat. Make an educated guess at what works by stepping in the shoes of those you hope to attract and use content to attract them. Link your efforts in one platform to those on your website and other platforms to create a seamless net which captures eyeballs and minds.

Whatever you do, never treat a medium as a standalone option. Never treat a platform as something so new you cannot get a handle on it (if that's the case you should not be there) and never transfer responsibility for the content you post to your public (you are the professional – behave like one).

Follow these rules and though there is as much chance that you will get it wrong as there is that you will get it right, you'll never be accused of not 'getting it'.

# ∎Chapter 7

## The Social Fabric

"**B**leeding, I called 999. A tired man told me to go home." So does Andrew Gilligan, a reporter for the *Telegraph*, begin his tale of being mugged during the London riots of summer 2011. The spark for the riots was a peaceful march on 6th August 2011 held in protest of the fatal Police shooting of Mark Duggan, a local figure with a shady past who was shot resisting arrest. Duggan had been shot just 48 hours earlier and the Police had managed to mishandle a whole host of communication opportunities which resulted in generating some tension with the local community.

How we go from there to the point that London is engulfed in riots, looting and burning buildings for five days and how other cities across England and the UK also experience bouts of rioting is an entirely different story. What is of note here is that this is the first case of rioting, on record, where social media played a vital part, both in its inception and spread and, again, in the aftermath when things returned to normal.

That, for us, is the really important lesson to look at because social media is only going to play a greater and greater role in future social developments and in the organisation of offline events and it may, even, force the shaping of social policies.

In order to understand why this is, it is important to understand technical concepts such as channel recognition, critical mass, market penetration, user experience and threshold usage barriers which are all factors involved in the uptake of anything, from best-selling books to popular sayings in films and TV serials which become part of everyday life.

Essentially in order for something to be adopted it is not enough for it to simply be there. We are all exposed to sufficient 'noise' as part of our everyday life to be largely immune to the excitement that something new generates.

So in order for us to actually make the conscious decision to become part of, let's say, a social network, or to adopt a particular type of technology there has to be sufficient uptake and publicity (for peer group pressure to kick in) and a sense of relative uniqueness when you are not doing what everybody else is. Social networks like Twitter and Facebook and the tools you need to make them work for you like smartphones, tablets and netbooks have reached just that stage of widespread adoption.

To really understand this consider that social networks do not offer anything new which we do not, already, do in the offline world. Nor do they offer anything which we have not done for thousands of years. The functionality they offer which helps us interact with each other, form groups, make new friends, share our interests, ideas and hobbies, and discover new information is powered by the fact that we have behaved like this for thousands of years. Although they have not really given us something new but social networks have given us something a lot more powerful in terms of ease of use, ease of access and depth of reach. Already we have started to see the effects of all this in business, businessmen and their ceaseless networking. Because social networks allow us to create online profiles which become an interpretable representation of who we are, the life we live and the country we are in, we have managed to create an online culture where we all ceaselessly peek over the barriers of the past, peering directly into each other's lives.

When you hear that just in Google+, a social network which took just over a month to acquire 40 million members, those who were active uploaded over three billion photographs, you begin to realise the power all this imagery has when it is taken as a collective. That amount of visual data has impact, it subtly invades and then sways hearts and minds, it can reinforce social values, foster new ideas, give rise to fresh ideals and that's without the ability of social networking to make country borders and geographical barriers temporarily vanish through the more direct medium of written and, in the case of Google+, video contact.

We already have seen the results.


## Social media as a catalyst

Revolutions, rarely start in big ways. They are revolutions because, they are the result of something small, gradually building up. They are the result of social pressure which mounts up against barriers until the barriers themselves, which have kept it back, begin to give and a point of no return is reached.

Working online I have come across 'world changing' technologies more times than I care to mention. The spread of computers was said to be enough to 'change the world', email was hailed as a 'communications breakthrough' and the web itself was slated to 'do away with national boundaries'. All of these have happened to some extent but the world did not change as a result. It just became different.

We used computers and connectivity to find different ways to work, for instance, so that we could work longer and harder, holding cybermeetings across timezones, outsourcing non-essential services to lower-cost economies and working productively round the clock.

We used the web to hire virtual assistants to reduce office overheads, and we each became entrepreneurs, using the virtual economy as our playground to set up new businesses, try different business models and pursue ideas which had been burning a hole in the back of our heads since the days before we could escape the nine-to-five cubicle hell.

While all of these changed something, they really changed so little that they changed almost nothing. Until now. Change is always defined by the unexpected or rather by the likelihood of the unexpected occurring.

The thing no one can predict is always a good indicator of a fundamental we have missed in our calculations. Social media provides the ingredient which often leads to the kind of unpredictability which is the hallmark of real change.

We have already seen how social media connects people and brands, how it allows companies to become more responsive to their customers and how it empowers consumers to express their opinions and interact with the companies they like.

Social media has given real meaning to the words 'brand ambassador' and 'audience interaction'. All of this we know and much of it we had forecast. None of it, however, is why social media is changing so much of the world we know.

As you are reading this much of the Middle East is in the grip of what has been called 'The Arab Spring'. Popular uprisings in Egypt, Tunisia, Libya and Syria are seeing trends for regime change and some form of democratization. This has been truly unexpected and it has been brought about by the catalyst action of social media. Here are three reasons why:

▸ **Social Media connects**. Once we overlook the functionality attributes and the 'bells and whistles' of every form of social media platform and social media channel we are left with their ability to help us do what human beings always do best: connect with each other. In the interaction there is a deep and often overlooked cross-fertilisation of ideas, thoughts and opinions. A true break down of national borders and cultural barriers. People in Pakistan get to see party pics from Frat Houses in the US. Repressed Tunisians find out, in passing, that UK wages are much higher than theirs for the exact same job. Egyptians freely talk to counterparts in the West and wonder why their lifestyles are so different.

I am painting here a picture with incredibly broad strokes but social change of the type we are witnessing in our times does not happen unless there is an accumulation of detail at a personal level which can bring about a tipping point which, in turn, reaches critical mass within a national pool. Social media allows connection across billions of lives on a one-to-one basis in a way which is totally new.

› **Social Media connects**. The connections social media allows us to make do not just run from the inside out (i.e. from a communications challenged society to the 'free world' and back) but also spread within. The Egyptian uprising would, arguably, have not taken place had not Facebook enabled groups of demonstrators within Egypt to communicate and become organised long before the authorities really understood what was happening. Social media has been instrumental in creating cohesion amongst disparate rebel groups in Libya and it has been used to communicate amongst them, and get organized, by the demonstrators in Syria. It has kept news and images coming out in real time, appearing on Twitter and Google+ and has maintained both the world's attention and momentum in movements which might otherwise have fizzed or been squashed by their own governments.

› **Social Media connects**. The very heavily publicised, 2011 street riots in London and several other UK cities would have received neither the world media attention they did nor the public opinion debate which they started had not the use of social media had made it possible to securely organize them in the first place and then publicise them in the second. Social media, like the

spinning jenny, is changing an entire industry and, as
the UK government's reactions to it shows (the UK
Parliament toyed with the possibility of shutting down
social media channels during times of national crisis), it
has not failed to produce its own special brand of
Luddites.

Like most profound changes social media works
at several different levels at once. For marketers and
marketing it represents a challenge and an opportunity.
The challenge is to foster true personal communication
with their potential audience and market to them as you
would market to friends. The opportunity is to finally
leave the 'clever gimmicks' of advertising behind and
put in place a marketing framework which works with
simple truths.

## Social Media is the new battleground

No new forum for communication which deserves the
mantle of being revolutionary can be complete without
its dark side.

In the "war against terror" social media takes
centre stage. To some extent that's to be expected. War
and terrorism have always used complex tactics of
information and misinformation to get their message
across and recruit followers.

In the past this was limited to moments of
sufficient public impact to warrant extensive news
coverage. This has now changed and social media is,
once again, responsible.

Ayman al-Zawahiri, the current head of al-
Qaeda, once remarked: "We are in a media battle for
hearts and minds." He did not know just how prophetic
his words were.

156

Al Qaeda is a strange organisation, attracting man whose private motives are as complex as their backgrounds. One of them was American born Anwar al-Awlaki whose sermons in a Falls Church mosque, in Virginia, had gained him a core following.

Anwar al-Awlaki was softly, spoken, charismatic, intense, as only people who follow a terrorist organisation frequently can be, and rose to become a senior Al Qaeda leader in Yemen. In a more conventional age his departure from the US would have isolated him from much of the world and made him relevant only locally and then only where organising incidents of terrorism were concerned.

This is not a conventional age any longer.

Fully aware of the impact of social media and its ability to reach an audience across timezones and national borders Anwar al-Awlaki kept a blog and was active on Facebook as well as a number of other social media platforms. More than that he was a master of social media interactions, understanding how to use the social media platform to propagate in an ever-widening net Al Qaeda's ideology.

"The internet has become a great medium for spreading the call of jihad and following the news of the mujahidin," Awlaki once wrote.

He encouraged supporters to become "internet mujahidin" by establishing discussion forums, sending out email blasts, posting or emailing jihadi literature and news, and setting up websites to distribute information.

Such was the reach of his influence through social media that CIA placed him as the man responsible for providing strategic and operational guidance to Umar Farouk Abdulmutallab, who is accused of trying to blow up Northwest Airlines Flight 253 on Christmas Day in 2009 with a bomb in his underwear. And it was Awlaki, again, who encouraged a US Army psychiatrist by the name of Maj Nidal Malik Hasan, to kill US soldiers, resulting, in November 2009, in Maj Hasan gunning down 13 people and wounding 43 others at Fort Hood, Texas.

Awlaki's success at spreading Al Qaeda ideology was the clearest indication yet that the US campaign against terrorism could not be won by drones alone. It has become a battle of ideas where social media was at the centre.

Ironically enough it was drones which drove the point about social media's effectiveness, firmly home. In September 30 2011 Anwar al-Awlaki became a casualty of war when his location came under a planned drone attack. With his demise Al Qaeda's social media strategy suffered a serious blow and much of its influence upon the Arab world suddenly began to wane.

A Pew Research Center report just a few months later indicated a changed picture with Al-Qaeda's popularity. Bereft of its social media master to continue to guide its publicity activities, the report showed that now only 2% of Muslims in Lebanon and 5% in Turkey expressed favourable views of al-Qaeda. In Jordan, a traditional Al-Qaeda hotbed, only 15% had a positive opinion of the organisation. The trend is unmistakable: Al-Qaeda, and its ideology, without a social media strategist have lost significant support.

The message is equally unmistakeable. Social media, for world leaders and governments now represents a genie which having granted them their wish for a means to communicate with their people during election campaigns is refusing to go back in the lamp and is giving the very same power to their electorates and opponents. It is eroding communication barriers which allowed 'controlled messages' to be sent out and it is allowing the message to simply find its way through the noise.

For companies, governments and brands, just like for Al-Qaeda, the pressure is on sustained, sustainable efforts. Social media is unforgiving. The moment you back away from your activities you create the impression that you are backing away from what you do, and that, usually, loses you followers, be they online customers, voters or would be recruits.

For the individual social media represents a real challenge when it comes to filtering out 'noise' and finding out what's real and pertinent to them at that particular moment in time. It also offers the opportunity to enjoy connectivity and interaction at an unprecedented level and with a newfound degree of immediacy which is having a continuous impact upon many other areas of our lives.

Where does that leave us now? The true impact of social media in marketing, communication, and gradual social change is something which I think we will not see until we see it. Much like 'The Arab Spring' change is happening right now in ways we cannot readily measure and therefore cannot easily predict. What we do know with some certainty however is that things are gradually changing and they will continue to change. The question remains the same for everyone: how fast do we change? And then, how far?

## Social Media is a uniting thread

We look to communication within a social setting, and communication within our social groups to do two things: to define us for what we are and then draw us together through shared values and a shared volume of information.

In this setting information is important because it becomes the subtle language we use to establish a common frame of reference for communication as well as a means to widen our horizons. In a pub setting situation and within small social groups information exchanged about hobbies, activities and, even, news helps us to establish common areas of interest, navigate away from potential social mine fields which may lead to arguments and form a commonly shared sense of identity.

In the social media age, social media itself is forming a thread which is creating a new social fabric, held together by a brand new set of shared values and ideas.

This, however, was not a thought which would have been going through Ramy Essam's mind on the 9 March 2011. At that time he was in a dark cell, surrounded by officers belonging to the military elite ruling in Egypt who were busy cutting his long hair with glass and preparing the wooden bats which they were going to beat him with.

Ramy Essam had become a symbol. An ordinary Egyptian student whose voice had made him the singer of the revolution in Egypt's Tahrir Square, he achieved an unusual honour.

160

Ramy's improvised songs and guitar playing had provided a focal point and had become the anthem which had held ordinary Egyptians together from January to March 2011, as they were attacked by thugs on camelback, hired by Egypt's ruling military elite.

What makes Ramy special is the same thing which makes the Egyptian uprising and the Arab Spring special: social media.

Quite unwittingly Ramy had become a social media hero. The entire Egyptian uprising, in a country where the military held complete control over all forms of communication and transportation, had been coordinated through Facebook. A social network whose servers could not be turned off and which, when examined by a bewildered Egyptian ruling elite, appeared to devolve into a mass of 'wow's', 'lol's' and cruder comments and banalities about ordinary things, had also become the conduit through which the Egyptian masses coordinated their protest, exchanged ideas and opinions and shared stories about Ramy and his songs.

This is the power of social media to appear, at close inspection, to be fragmented, as bewildering and unfocused as day-dreaming and yet, collectively, provide a means of multi-way communication which can be adapted to almost anything.

In the case of the Egyptian uprising, in a model which was to be copied by residents in Tunisia, Lybia, Syria and, even, Saudi Arabia, Arabs took to the web, bypassing the stringent checks and controls of their own culture and their own societies and forming a grassroots movement which has brought about the transformation of countries which no one thought would be transformed any time this century.

Social media, then, it appears, has contributed significantly to the downfall of restrictive Arab regimes and, we know that it has become a major channel for dissidents from countries like Russia, China and Iran to air their views and get information out of the country.

For a totalitarian regime of any sort, social media has to be the equivalent of garlic to a vampire (or vervain for *Vampire Diaries* fans). Its ability to take the establishment by surprise lies not so much in the way it makes those in power suddenly accountable to their people, though this is definitely one of its characteristics, as in the fact that those in power suddenly find themselves faced with a media platform they are powerless to control.

In view of that, this official statement should then come as no surprise: *"So we are working with the police, the intelligence services, and industry to look at whether it would be right to stop people from communicating via these websites and services when we know they are plotting violence, disorder and criminality."*

The statement, worthy of any head of state in a totalitarian regime country, was made by none other than British Prime Minister, David Cameron, addressing the House of Commons during an emergency recall of the Parliament, following the London riots in August 2011.

It's true that rioters (and looters) used Facebook and Twitter to communicate nationally and they then used the encrypted, secure Blackberry Network to instant message each other using BlackBerry Messenger (BBM).

162

The Prime Minister, addressing his peers, and sounding bewildered said how anyone watching the riots would be "struck by how they were organised via social media".

If we are to get into the nitty-gritty of the reasons for the riots across the UK (and the shooting of Mark Duggan was only the flashpoint) they lie much deeper and, I suspect, upon close inspection offer many similarities to what we see in Egypt, Tunisia, Russia.

The reasons we are looking for would have to be found not on the use of social media, as the British Prime Minister, somewhat disingenuously suggested, but in deep social inequalities, neglect and a misplaced culture of entitlement which has created a wellhead of disenfranchised youths across the nation. This is as strong a sentiment in England, where there are social groups which sense they are isolated from the system which governs their country, as it is across the Arab world, where Arab youths feel forgotten and unlistened to by their own, seemingly less-enlightened regimes.

Certainly, in this case, the looting and violence being witnessed in London's Totenham, was less idealistic and far less righteous than the events transpiring in Tahrir Square, in Egypt. Yet it is interesting to see two things here which reflect a certain degree of similarity. First that liberal, open-minded, deeply democratic Britain when faced with a communication channel it could not shut off and which its government could not control, suddenly, sounded as desperate, ignorant and authoritarian as the countries it has for years now accused for trying to censor the internet. Second, that, social media acted as a thread, pulling together a new social fabric and authoring a new way of doing things. The youths in Totenham may have been destructive and perhaps self-serving in their looting, but deep down they had more in common with the masses in Tahrir Square than may at first meet the eye.

As former Mayor of London and Labour politician, Ken Livingstone put it, the rioters in London were those who "feel no one at the top of society, in government or City Hall, cares about them or speaks for them".

If social media can be a thread which pulls together the new kind of world we are creating out of our voices, made suddenly louder and more potent, its ability to act for bad as well as for good has to depend upon what we do at a personal level.

Just two days after the worst rioting England had seen since the 80s, millions of people were signing up on Facebook supporting the police and their handling of the riots, and organising through Twitter operation 'fightback' where local communities came together to help clean up the streets from the debris.

The Arab Spring and the UK riots acted as spotlights. The first made social media (and Facebook in particular) a darling, while the second demonized it, casting it in a much more lurid light.

Both cases highlight the fact that we are living in a time of social change. We feel that our world is somehow broken, that those who are in positions of authority no longer listen to us and that those we rely upon to govern us no longer know quite what they are doing. We want to do something (sometimes anything) to try and fix this disconnect, or to make those who are in power suddenly sit up and take notice.

Just after the London riots happened social media played a much larger, global role, in something much bigger and (this time) more noble than looting.

## Social Media is a podium

As I was writing this book I came across a song in my collection from my youth by Aerosmith called *Living on the Edge* the lyrics of which start with:

> There's somethin' wrong with the world today
> I don't know what it is
> Something's wrong with our eyes
>
> We're seeing things in a different way
> And God knows it ain't His
> It sure ain't no surprise...

The reason this is pertinent here is because it aptly captures a sentiment many of us have had for some time now.

Ever since the 9/11 World Trade Center attack in 2001, people I talked to across different industries and positions have had a sense that something is not quite right. When questioned many say that it's a sense that the world is changing in unquantifiable ways and we are heading towards something new, exciting and (as these things usually have it) painful in the experience of the transition period. Others say that they think the world is not working quite the way it should and it needs something to help fix it.

What that something might have been, could have been, in 2001 was impossible to tell and in 2007, a full six years later, we still had nothing concrete to offer. Struck by the fact that so many different people recounted this feeling and felt it strongly enough to share it with me, a relative stranger, made me incorporate it in many of my talks and presentations.

Truthfully though this is not really a new feeling. We all start out wanting to change the world, regardless, and in the end we settle for the world changing us (or at least putting a stop to our desire for change). The reason this happens is not because our ideals die or our ideas change. No, something else happens which is subtle and gradual and which works on all of us regardless. In the process of 'growing up', our picture of how complex the world really is becomes fleshed out and we begin to realise that we, as individuals, are rendered ineffectual by the sheer scale of things.

Faced by a world which appears to be a massive, slowly churning juggernaut, we realise that alone we can accomplish almost nothing. When we are in a group and have to communicate a thought or an idea we strive to, somehow, create the grounds necessary for the group to understand our vision, coalesce around it with a single, clear purpose and then think how it can act.

While we know that in a group situation this can be accomplished and we can, somehow, get followers who will share this vision of ours, whatever it may be, there is a small catch. We know that even if we happen to be *that* charismatic the task of getting others to listen to us is still daunting and fraught with risks of being ridiculed, ostracized or simply labelled as a loon, which is why we do not even try.

Yet, the desire to change things, to somehow leave a mark on the world, however small, is universal. Part of it is expressed in graffiti, vandalism and small anonymous acts of kindness. The reason we are all capable of these things is because each of us is exposed, more or less, to the same stimuli in our world. We all swim in the same pool, but we just happen to each swim there alone.

Without technology or rather without our current level of technology the only way to achieve anything would be to willingly accept the collectivization of our identities into groups led by a commonly accepted 'higher authority'. While this may be an obvious way of harnessing individuals in order to achieve a common goal, as Communism so aptly demonstrated, it is an arrangement which is so vulnerable to abuse of power that it is hardly a guaranteed way to bring about any kind of meaningful change.

Social media changes all of this by breaking down the barriers separating individuals while still managing to maintain their distinct identity. It allows 'small' individual acts of communication, from a Tweet, to a Like to the expression of an idea on Google+ to begin to act on the collective through further interaction. This suddenly provides not just total freedom of expression, several degrees removed from the awkward perceived judgment of face-to-face communication, bu tit also provides a pulpit and a channel, all wrapped up into one allowing thoughts and ideas the room to run, truly free and maybe, even, a little wild.

Something you post on a social network becomes, in a sense, immortal. It exists forever, it can take on a life of its own and, because the population density of social media networks, and their popularity, act as funnels, bringing groups of disparate and frequently isolated people together it increases the likelihood of any particular post has of falling upon the right pair of ears and act as a catalyst in ways which cannot be foreseen.

On September 17th 2011 the unpredictable improbability which comes from the build up of social pressure took very real form. A group of protesters peacefully took over Zuccotti Park, near Wall Street in protest to the inequalities they were perceiving in finance and politics, in the immediate, physical world around them.

What should have been an ill-conceived action by a fringe group brought to the very edge of their tolerance by personal financial pressures due to the global credit crunch suddenly, through exposure on social media platforms, became a rallying point. It became a reason to think deeper and more profoundly about our financial system than ever before and it fuelled the sense that "something had to be done".

This gave birth to the slogan "we are the 99%" and led to impromptu, similar actions which were held in Singapore, Portland, Toronto and London. The protests were disorganised in their demands and lacked a single cohesive vision. There was no leader. There was no manifesto, there were deep cultural and language divides. What did become painfully clear however was that running through the protests was a sentiment, spread through social networks, which was suddenly global. The feeling of discontent and the sense of social injustice which fuelled it had become a unifying thread running across countries and cultures, bound by the sense that the mere vocalisation of it would have some effect.

The dynamics underlying the spread of the message of the 99ers and its appeal to those who came across it are complicated. There is no denying however that without a social media platform to work through there would have been no spreading of the word, or the sentiments the 99ers represented. There would have been no public support, or thinking about their demands in other quarters. There would have been no build up in social pressure, discussions, expectations and dissections of why this was happening, what it meant and what we should each do about it.

Almost certainly there also would have been no public announcements from people like global financier Warren Buffet who argued publicly for higher taxes for the wealthy in an open letter to the *New York Times*, or British business secretary, Vince Cable, who not only expressed sympathy for the St Paul protesters in London in an article on the popular British newspaper, *The Telegraph*, but also vowed to work to curb the pay of those who caused the financial crisis in the first place.

These are results which make sense on a personal basis. They are totally logical when we really think about our systems and institutions and the way they work (or not) and they are justified in the context of our trying to fix them. They are also the kind of results which, in the pre-social media age would simply not have been even conceivable let alone possible.

The very fact that a peaceful occupation of a few hundred square metres by a bunch of people, many of whom might actually belong to the fringes of mainstream society, has begun the process of change in our institutions of government and financing and may be the first step towards curbing and humanising some of the worst excesses of capitalism, is a telling blow for what I can only regard as the ability of the web to provide power to the voice of the individual, through social media. Why? How?

These are the questions which are at the very heart of the social media revolution. Before the internet, a challenge, any challenge to a sacred cow (and we had herds of them, everywhere) was greeted with the same close-minded, protectionist, knee-jerk reaction the Church reserved for Galileo Galilei in the 16th century when he dared to suggest that the Earth was not the centre of the universe.

When the internet first happened, many of us who worked at the very edge of the technological wave, seeing and sensing the potential it contained, hailed it (mostly in private) as the means through which each person could be made to matter again.

At the time we did not know how this could happen. Without the social media platform to humanise interactions we were left with the sense that we had stepped onto a vast global stage, it was there. We just lacked the mechanism to make it do what we wanted it to, so we remained lone voices, with a little more hope but lacking the means to connect.

The mechanism we lacked back then is now here. It is easily and freely available to me, you and anyone driven by a sense that there is something to do, something to say, maybe even something to change in the world. Anyone can create a Facebook Page, a Google

Plus Circle, a social media platform presence and broadcast thoughts, ideas and opinions, from there.

I am not, here, suggesting that this, somehow is a golden age of 'good' where only those with hallowed intentions or socially good sentiments will get to be heard, quite the opposite in fact, freedom of expression and the power to use it means just that. When your soapbox can now make you heard across the globe the fact is that almost everyone with half a notion and the urge to voice it will want to do so.

That's what makes this exciting. We are entering into a new age. An age where the voice and the noise, the idea and the signal all get to get mixed up and interact. It is a meld the likes of which the world has never seen before and one from which we can only emerge culturally and intellectually enriched, regardless.

When I was at university there was a slogan making the rounds on the back of a dorm sticker: "You think education is expensive?" it asked, "try ignorance". It stayed with me throughout my adult life, made me want to usually go to great lengths to spread knowledge and storm bastions where special interest groups played closed shop, keeping the masses out of their own little closely guarded universe of knowledge.

Social media may not be the magic bullet which instantly makes all the world's entrenched woes vanish but it certainly is a means of calling for and providing greater transparency in every sphere of human activity, than ever before.

This can only be good.

When I voiced this with some friends, a little before the idea for this book came together, one of them said that "Social media is Pandora's box. All the ills are now flying out."

It was a good point, well made. It changes nothing of what I said. If true, amongst the myriads of ills loosed upon the world, social media, like Pandora's box, also lets out hope. But I believe social media is not quite like that. It's not an unleashing of all sorts of possibilities for dissent and mischief which, before it came along, had been safely contained.

Social media is more like a flashlight. Before we switched it on we were unaware of what was going on in the shadows, hidden by darkness. Its beam of publicity, now, makes us see things which before we could only suspect. And once we see, we are left with little choice but to take action.

## Social media is changing us

I began this chapter wanting to show just how social media is changing our world, providing pressures which did not exist before and which are causing our real-life institutions, our very society, in fact, to change.

Such change is, out of necessity, slow to take place. Sometimes infuriatingly so, but it is happening. Of even greater interest is the fact that social media is changing us, not just in the way we think about things, or how we communicate our ideas to the world or even how find out information relevant to us. It is doing all those things, certainly, but now, it is changing us physically.

It is changing our brains.

In the 70s, which is not that long ago really, the accepted dogma was that whatever smarts we were born with that was it. We could only hope to capitalize on them until our mid-twenties and then consign ourselves to a lengthy period of decline.

We know that now to be bunk. Our brainpower can be made to improve and we can become smarter (or dumber should we so choose to) and our brains are far more malleable, responsive and adaptable than our bodies, and social media is rewiring them.

In October 2011 a group of researchers at the University College London, published the results of a survey of adult users of social networks in the *Proceedings of the Royal Society B*.

"The increasing ubiquity of web-based social networking services is a striking feature of modern human society. The degree to which individuals participate in these networks varies substantially for reasons that are unclear. Here, we show a biological basis for such variability by demonstrating that quantitative variation in the number of friends an individual declares on a web-based social networking service reliably predicted grey matter density in the right superior temporal sulcus, left middle temporal gyrus and entorhinal cortex." Cited the study as part of its summary.

In plain English, after using MRI scans on the brains of 165 adults, the researchers concluded that those who had a number of Facebook friends above 150 (the Dunbar Number[1]) showed significantly higher grey

---

[1] Robin Dunbar is a professor of Evolutionary Anthropology at Oxford University who has conducted research revealing that while social networking sites allow us to maintain more relationships, the number of meaningful friendships is the same as it has been

matter density in the amygdala, an area the study says was already known to be linked to real world social network size, as well as in other regions including the right entorhinal cortex, which is associated with memory.

"Taken together, our findings show that the number of social contacts declared publicly on a major web-based social networking site was strongly associated with the structure of focal regions of the human brain," the researchers concluded.

While, at this early point of the research on the neurological impact of social networks, we are looking at a chicken and egg kind of question on whether an increase in grey matter density is caused by excessive

---

throughout history, and that number, which has become known as the Dunbar Number, is 150.

Dunbar's theory known as "Dunbar's number" was developed in the 1990s and its premise is that the size of our neocortex — the part of the brain used for conscious thought and language — limits us to managing social circles of around 150 friends, no matter how sociable we are or how sociable technology allows us to become.

The 150 people in this naturally defined 'tribe' are, to all intents and purposes part of our real, modern tribe, because each of them is a person whom we know how they relate to every other friend in the group. These 150 people are people, according to the Dunbar Theory, which you care about and contact at least once a year.

Dunbar derived the limit from studying social groupings in a variety of societies — from neolithic villages to modern office environments. He found that people tended to self-organise in groups of around 150 because social cohesion begins to deteriorate as groups become larger.

social networking or it happens to be a feature of those who excel in it, the informal indications tend to argue towards the former rather the latter.

Not too long ago in a talk to a group of managers eager to understand how search could benefit their business I explained that the internet is not just changing the way business operates on the web but the very way we use our brains, which is the first clue they need to know when they are thinking about business and search.

The fact is that technology probably started to change us the moment we bent down to pick up a rock and weigh it up for throwing. As humans we have the ability to use technology to short-circuit biology and evolution, augment our strengths and lessen our weaknesses and the way we use the web and search is no exception.

Much has been made of a study recently published in *Science* which looked at the effect search engines are having on the way we use our brains to store our memories. Although the study implies that by relying on search engines to find things for us we are giving up the ability to remember facts which matter it is wrong in its assumption.

We live in a world which can be eminently hostile. A sudden drop from a moderate height or a drop in temperature by a few degrees can kill us. The summer 2011 heat wave which hit America and its fatal effects makes a compelling argument about our vulnerability to our environment.

Having neither very sharp teeth nor long claws and with muscles which can lose up to 50% of their power over a 24-hour period of inactivity we are ill-

suited for fighting anything bigger than a large house
cat, and even then we might be challenged.

Yet, we have managed to climb to the top of the
food chain and become the apex predator on a planet
whose environment challenges us, almost, at every step
but we have done so because we rely so heavily on
technology. It should come, then, as no surprise that
search engines, the starting point of the day for a large
percentage of this planet's population, should have such
an impact on our behaviour.

Search engine optimisers have known all along
that human behaviour is in adaptive mode when it
comes to search and the web. Anecdotal examples show
that many of us rely on Google's ability to auto-correct
words and suggest the correct spelling and, therefore
use the search engine not only to find items we are not
100% sure how they are spelled, but also to often correct
our own spelling.

When Google Instant was implemented, for
example, it was a piece of programming designed to
suggest possible search queries based on anonymously
accrued search results. The intention, from Google, was
to help shave micro-seconds off the typing of search
queries, improving the end-user experience. The search
algorithm did not change and the way websites were
being indexed did not change. Yet, this relatively simple
change, presented SEOs with a major challenge.

As people chose the immediate option on offer
and clicked on the Google-served suggestions websites
which were either not popular enough or not optimised
enough in relation to specific search terms saw their
traffic dip sharply. This made a first page on Google
position the only Google ranking that mattered.

As web users we are constantly locked into adaptive learning behaviour. The web is changing at such a ferocious pace that functionality and design develop in a complex feedback cycle where we take the technology developers create (and which websites use) and through usage create a demand for the next wave of developments.

Adaptive learning not only makes us enthusiastic early adopters of everything the web has to offer but it allows us to seek innovative ways to use it which will offer us some kind of nearly instant gain.

Transactive memory is the mind-trick that's always 'on'. Basically, the brain remembers where to get information it needs (and how) rather than bothering to remember all the information it needs. In the past we would have our trusted tribal or local community sources (the 'fixer' or the 'source'). Today we rely on Google's ability to search the web and the web's capacity for storing an infinite amount of information.

This may well mean that without our plugged-in connections we are less intelligent but it also means that by avoiding filling our heads with clutter we are able to think in a wider, more analytical perspective which should, in principal, help expand our understanding of the world and lead to better decision planning.

So, it is this collision between the technical and the human which creates the crucible out of which so many new possibilities arise and so much excitement is generated, The web, clearly, is not just driving business and information, it is also shaping the evolution of human intellect, broadening our store of knowledge and providing us with the capability to better plan our future.

Social media is only accelerating this process by involving in in-depth use of the web and its technologies, people who might otherwise not have spent as much time being online. The result of this is that we all find ourselves working in a shared environment which exposes us to similar stimuli and similar experiences and which contributes to a new form of shared perspectives and shared values.

If my theory is right, then we should start to see evidence of the influence of social media not just in riots and demonstrations and the peaceful occupation of landmarks in an attempt to reshape public policy, but in other spheres of influence where unlike the examples I have just mentioned, social media may not be expected to have any impact at all and for which there is no tradition of offline world activity.

These are the areas we are going to examine next.

# ■Chapter 8
## Science and the Social Web

F or more than a decade, an international team of scientists has been trying to figure out the detailed molecular structure of a protein-cutting enzyme from an AIDS-like virus found in rhesus monkeys. Such enzymes, known as retroviral proteases, play a key role in the virus' spread, and if medical researchers can figure out their structure, they could conceivably design drugs to stop the virus in its tracks. The strategy has been compared to designing a key to fit one of Mother Nature's locks.

The problem is that enzymes are far tougher to crack than your typical lock. There are millions of ways that the bonds between the atoms in the enzyme's molecules could twist and turn. To design the right chemical key, you have to figure out the most efficient, lowest-energy configuration for the molecule, the one that Mother Nature herself came up with.

You'd think that given the problem and sufficient computer power this should be a straightforward problem to crack. It isn't.

179

Computers are great at powering their way through number-crunching equations which is why they can now beat us at Chess, but when it comes to spatial reasoning we are still light-years ahead of them.

In September 20th 2011 a small piece of internet history was made when it was announced that videogamers playing a game version of the molecular structure problem which had baffled scientists for years, had solved in it less than 10 days.

Published in the journal *Nature Structural & Molecular Biology*, the study under the name of *Crystal structure of a monomeric retroviral protease solved by protein folding game players* explained how the problem had been codified and put online for an online community of gamers playing Foldit, a collaborative structural manipulation game, to take a shot at.

## Crowdsourcing and social media

Crowdsourcing, like many of the aspects of social media we look at, is not new either. Behind it is the belief that the wisdom of crowds is bigger and better than the wisdom of the individual (in the past) and the knowledge of machines (today). Democracy, in a sense, is based upon crowdsourcing and so is Google's TipJar (http://goo.gl/MmBI) which uses the wisdom offered by the crowds to create a database of tips to specific problems which save time and money.

What is new, here, is that the ease with which some problems can be re-stated in a social media environment can lead to some incredible results.

The AIDS enzyme molecular-structure problem, for instance, might have been capable of being solved by crowds at the very beginning of the century, when it surfaced, but back then we lacked two crucial elements, both of which are at the very heart of the words 'social' and 'media'. First the ability to be transparent (which scientist worth his research grant would be willing to admit defeat and ask for help back then?) and secondly the ability to translate scientific concepts into a more socially-acceptable light-hearted principle, like a game.

The gamers who solved the puzzle might have been aware that they were helping crack a scientific mystery which had resisted the attempts of some of the best minds in the field for over a decade, but to them it was a game where they had to manipulate virtual molecular structures that look like multicolored, curled-up Tinkertoy sets. The virtual molecules follow the same chemical rules that are obeyed by real molecules. When someone playing the game comes up with a more elegant structure that reflects a lower energy state for the molecule, his or her score goes up. If the structure requires more energy to maintain, or if it doesn't reflect real-life chemistry, then the score is lower.

Simple, right?

Yet it has taken us ten years to get here from there and the reason is obvious. Social may be the ingredient which transforms everything but embracing it requires a fantastic investment in trust and a willingness to get out of the traditional, compartmentalised mentality which keeps us captive within our narrow worlds, and helps to hyper-inflates the opinion we have of ourselves and what we do.

In a way we have seen the likes of something like this before.

Back in the 18th century, Georgian England underwent a rapid explosion of knowledge and an expansion of its territories the likes of which had never been seen before.

Advancement in fields of knowledge then, came from people outside the narrow, hallowed, feted, professional groups and closed societies of the day. For instance, George Harrison, a clockmaker, solved the naval navigation issue and the calculation of longitude, which had been costing countless lives and lost ships. William Smith, the father of Geology, was practically self-educated, and Christopher Saxton, who produced the first accurate Atlas, was just a draper.

The Georgian era, was perhaps the first time in history where we saw the concerted rise of the citizen-scientist. Ground-breaking theories and many advances came, during this time, from the most unexpected quarters. Many of these were proposed by self-educated laymen who had the advantage of working outside the established boundaries of professional knowledge, and were therefore not bound by the limitations which those imposed.

The Georgian era, in turn, gave way to the Victorians, which gave us photography, telephones, electric light bulbs, stamps, the first one-piece toilet and cars.

We frequently like to say that history repeats itself but that's never true. History practically never repeats itself but our actions and reactions frequently lead us into patterns of behaviour which are roughly cyclical in nature. So it is truer, though far less poetic, to say that history leads us into similar circumstances with those of the past but which are sufficiently different as to be uniquely ours.

Our time is no exception. As social media is eroding the traditional barriers between professions it now leads to what is perhaps the best of all possible worlds: an opening up of professions in a way akin to that witnessed during Georgian times which was subsequently followed by the avalanche of advances and fresh discoveries which marked the Victorian era.

Proof of this is provided by some mind-boggling examples. A Dutch artist by the name of Jalila Essaïdi, inspired by transgenic experiments, used social media to collaborate with a cell biologist by the name of Abdoelwaheb El Ghalbzouri. Jalila wanted to produce an example of a spider silk/human skin hybrid as part of an art project. The result of the combined knowledge and expertise of these two very different people ended up being a blended spider silk and human skin product which proved to be a super-strong material that is three times stronger than Kevlar and which can stop a bullet at half its regular speed.

Scientists have hailed this as a breakthrough and are working on perfecting it to a point where it will be 22 times stronger than Kevlar, in which case its applications in a wide variety of situations where lightweight, ultra-strong protection is required will be almost endless.

The case of Jalila and her unintentional scientific breakthrough perfectly illustrates what happens when you cross-pollinate ideas from different disciplines, unfetter the imagination and harness the human passion for creativity with the purpose to extend knowledge.

The results obtained from these early successes in the social media field are beginning to show just what is possible.

## Social media and education

It is entirely possible, for instance, to take a new social approach to learning hard sciences at school, using a collaborative approach and the principles of gamefication, applied to problem solving.

This will not just unlock new ways of thinking but it will also unlock new ways of learning. Particularly when, through the application of genuine knowledge sharing in a group environment we succeed in unleashing the power of groupthink while still promoting the individuality of the person.

This kind of re-thinking of how we approach work-related problems does not involve new skills but it does require a new mind set. For instance, the team of players which solved the AIDS enzyme question communicated via chat, worked collaboratively and individually and each individual's contribution was marked and, since this was a game, a score was allocated to them.

This methodology of working is one which takes engagement within a group and the work itself to entirely new levels. Widespread adoption of the principle at enterprise level, for instance, would require a deep rethinking about how we relate to work and this can only start at the level of education when the foundations are laid.

We are fast approaching the moment when we will return to the Georgian era citizen-scientist with the commensurate creation of a new kind of scientist and a new kind of science. Social media is not just responsible for the erosion of barriers vertically so that science becomes more accessible to the public at large which now get a real chance to participate. It also works in eroding barriers horizontally, with scientific disciplines suddenly getting the chance to interact with each other and share both theories and knowledge in a way which in the past was simply not feasible.

This is new ground for everyone and how we handle it will depend upon our willingness to be bolder and experiment to see what works.

When it comes to education it is telling perhaps that despite its importance in national politics and despite the fact that globally, in advanced nations, we have spent untold billions of dollars on different models, there is still no single country which can be held up as a shining paradigm that works.

I used to think that this is because education is complicated and we just need more time to get it right. But now I could easily argue that the model we are trying to apply is fundamentally flawed, and the millions we spend each year are there to help us shoehorn it into something which it shouldn't be.

Boston College, psychology professor, Peter Gray, who has specialised in developmental and evolutionary psychology, believes the mismatch in educational spending and the results we receive in return is due to an evolutionary mismatch.

Gray believes that part of the problem with education is that our much older and more deeply entrenched hunter-gatherer instincts are at odds with our much more recently acquired farming-orientated society ones:

"...the means by which children became educated in hunter-gatherer cultures were the opposite of the means by which we try to educate children in our schools today. One of the most cherished values of all band hunter-gatherer societies that have ever been studied by anthropologists is freedom. Hunter-gatherers believed that it is wrong to coerce a person to do what the person doesn't want to do — and they considered children to be people. They rarely even made direct suggestions, because that might sound like coercion. They believed that people, on their own initiative, would learn to contribute to the welfare of the band, because they would see the wisdom of doing so and experience the joy of it."

Apart from the fact that Gray here argues for a model which Gore Associates (the Gore Tex company) has successfully applied to the workplace[2] he is also arguing against the use of technology (and pretty much anything else) to force children to learn in what must clearly be an unnatural environment.

Evidence that he may be right is provided by a bold experiment carried out by the Kyrene School District (a group of 25 schools in Arizona, US) which has won awards and delivered impressive results with its innovative use of technology in the classroom to foster education and create highly motivated students.

---

[2] Gore Associates only hire 150 people per plant (the Dunbar number). Once hired no one tells you what to do and it is left up to you to find the means through which you can become a valuable member of the group, contributing positively to it.

In a revealing article published in the *New York Times* in September, 2011 a group of seventh graders studying Shakespeare's *As You Like It* were seen to take a less traditional approach to it: "In this technology-centric classroom, students are bent over laptops, some blogging or building Facebook pages from the perspective of Shakespeare's characters. One student compiles a song list from the Internet, picking a tune by the rapper Kanye West to express the emotions of Shakespeare's lovelorn Silvius."

The emphasis here is on social media and technology used to provide greater freedom. As the *Times* article read: *"The digital push here aims to go far beyond gadgets to transform the very nature of the classroom, turning the teacher into a guide instead of a lecturer, wandering among students who learn at their own pace on Internet-connected devices."*

Will it work? Will such controlled, but much freer approach to education, enabled by the use of technology and social media interaction (using Facebook, Twitter and Google+ to gauge interest in what students create and to generate further interactivity) succeed in providing students who are better at learning and more adaptable in the workplace?

When I was studying Chemical Engineering one of our more enlightened professors once stunned us by telling the class that everything we were learning was already obsolete and if we were serious about finding work we needed some hands-on work experience in a real factory setting.

He was right of course and his comment can easily be applied to almost any format of education we have today. Amidst reports in plateauing results in exams across most nations of the developed world, experiments like that of the Kyrene School District may provide a way of creating a new kind of educated professional. One who is at home in the ever changing environment of the web, who thinks nothing of changing disciplines mid-stride, altering career focus or picking up new skills a dozen times in their working life and one who feels that flexibility in learning and the freedom to generate true value for the social group are the most prized assets he can offer.

## Change your mind

What's needed here then is a change of mind. Whenever I talk to business groups about social media and what it can do I always make a point of stressing that social media is not another corporate media channel and to try and use it as such will only backfire.

It is the same in science and the same in education and it will be the same in practically every aspect of human communication in which now 'social' and 'media' come together (and yes that includes news gathering and even politics).

What's required is the ability to converse with, rather than talk to, those you deal with on an equal basis, ready to admit mistakes when they are made, and being prepared to explain motives and drives, when asked.

Traditionally such admissions and such questioning were seen as part of a challenge against authority. We do not live in traditional times any more. We should not be trapped in thinking and behaving like we do.

# ■Chapter 9
## Putting Social Media in Perspective

---

This entire book is about something revolutionary. A new way of doing things and getting far better results for less than ever before. There is an inherent trap here.

Social media marketing has gone from being the preserve of web-savvy marketers who could see that eyeballs on a brand or a product offered the potential to eventually increase market share, to being the darling of the press and almost every company 'out there' who suddenly feels the need to jump on the bandwagon.

This has also created a culture where social media marketing is something suddenly being offered by the world and his brother as online marketers of every description hurry to jump on before the train leaves the station. This is exactly where the trap is.

Social media is so popular because it appears easy to do. After all there is no rocket science involved in putting hashtags on Twitter, getting some 'Likes' on Facebook or seeing the +1 counter rise on Google Plus.

Now, here's the catch, even finely tuned social media marketing campaigns, carried out by experts, provide no hard correlation between social media marketing and sales. The number of these is finite and relatively rare.

The majority of media marketing campaigns I see are either ill-conceived or poorly executed, or both. Take, for instance, the very recent and very public social media disaster of Unilever's Ragu social media campaign which used a video with last-century, defining stereotypes to launch a Twitter campaign (because Ragu does social media, right?). In their effort to get noticed, Ragu's PR team spammed the Twitter accounts of male Twitter power-users and raised the ire of many of them who blogged their annoyance firstly because they were spammed, and secondly because they were being portrayed as stereotypical Neolithic dads whose families hated them getting mixed up in the kitchen (which is where Ragu stepped in to save the day). The culmination of it was a grassroots Twitter counter-campaign which centred around the sentiment: *'Ragu hates Dads'*.

Obviously they did not intend to create that reaction, but as any journalist worth his salt knows and as any social media manager will tell you every reaction is good and it creates an opportunity to win 'hearts and minds'. Ragu, to stick with the current example, blew even this opportunity by accusing in their Tweets, critical posts as "lacking balance". When called to task over it they simply shut up.

What all this illustrates is that what is apparently easy to do in terms of execution, actually is not. I consider strumming an acoustic guitar a fairly easy

190

thing to do also, but going from that strumming to producing the kind of tune which will make people around me stop what they are doing and take notice and then raise a clap when I am done takes finesse, talent, sensitivity and damn hard work.

Social media marketing is no exception. Funnily enough I saw the same Bell curve of popularity take off with SEO at the beginning of 2008 with just about anybody out there offering "to SEO your website" and it is only when we got down to needing meaningful results and bottom-line orientated numbers that the inevitable shakeout began to happen.

It is the same for social media. To say that it is difficult to quantify results is no excuse. The moment you apply any kind of social media marketing you need to have a clear goal in mind and a means of measuring how successful your efforts are.

## Social media is still new

The media attention on social media is approximately four years old. Social media, as a term we understand as well as an activity for connecting with friends and sharing information through online platforms is barely seven years old. Sometimes it is frightfully easy to lose sight of the wood for the trees.

The Pew Internet & American Life Project, an independent research organisation, released some data in September 2011 which revealed that despite its popularity social media is still trumped by email and search.

The figures showed that 92% of adults use email, with 61% using it on a typical day. But what's most worth paying attention to is the fact that, despite the significant growth experienced in social media usage over the past several years, email and search are still the most popular online activities.

Why? Understanding this simple question is crucial to crafting any kind of communication or marketing strategy which involves social media. Let's examine the way each is used.

First let's take email. Now an old and incredibly enough, traditional, means of communicating online, email is still the primary means of personal, one-to-one communication. The majority of business deals still start with email, and its ease of use and seemingly private nature make it a natural extension of how we view personal communication. Statistics, extrapolations and counting by Radicati Group, a Palo Alto based technology market research company, taken from April 2010 estimate the number of emails sent per day (in that year) to be around 294 billion. That's 294 billion messages per day which means that more than 2.8 million emails are sent every second and some 90 trillion emails are sent per year.

Then there is search. Comscore, a leader in measuring the digital world estimates that Google serves 34,000 searches per second worldwide, that's 2 million per minute, 121 million per hour; 3 billion per day or when you start to round the figures a little, 88 billion per month.

When compared to these numbers social media which features in website reports and magazines for its inability to still be adequately quantified, delivers a tiny portion of the bulk of communication. This is not a comment on its efficiency. Quite the contrary as a matter of fact. Content delivered over any social media channel has a far greater chance of being discovered and going viral than content in any other channel (the exception being perhaps the email exchange between Claire Swire and Bradley Chait, in December 2000, involving a private sexual act, which upon being forwarded by the latter to a couple of his friends made the circumnavigation of the globe, was featured on the UK national news and became an example for the need of employee email training for every UK firm, all within 24 hours).

So why, will you ask, is social media not beating email and search? After all it is far more engaging, interactive and entertaining.

The reasons lie in its very strengths and online user psychology. While social media may be the way we discover content and communicate when we are off work mode, when working or actively thinking about work, email, with its more targeted approach and more private nature, is deemed better. There is less distraction to sidetrack us and fewer opportunities for our attention to wander.

Then, search is the primary tool of choice which leads to the discovery of relevant content.

This is an important lesson to take on board because search and email usage are not likely to be knocked off their perch by social media. If anything, social media, itself, becomes important exactly because when content is socialised correctly it is easier to find in search.

So, you may well ask at this point, why all the fuss? Why is social media so prominently featured in reports and discussed so widely?

Social media, for all its apparent weakness when compared to email and search does what email and search cannot do: it helps shape perception, it helps create social cohesion, it helps shape ideas, it helps share ideals, it helps us to create an impression of the world which otherwise would have been impossible to create and because it is engaging and entertaining it does so subtly, in small ways which accumulate and have, eventually, significant impact.

Social media sharing and social media interaction are like ice and snow accumulating above a slope. For the most part they are pretty to look at and fun to deal with. Sometimes though, as Tahrir Square and the Arab Spring have demonstrated, the pressure goes past a critical point and an avalanche is unleashed.

# ■Chapter 10
## The Internet of Things

No book on social media and the social media mind would be complete without at least a look at a future which might be just round the corner. A future where social media communication happens not just between people but also between cars and home appliances and cars and people and home appliances and people, like your car talking to your Facebook friends or your fridge letting everyone on Twitter know what you shop.

Excited? Scared? Confused? You should be all of those things.

Most of the internet, right now, works on a standard called IPv4. BecauseIPv4 uses 32-bit (four-byte) addresses, which limits the address space we have got to the point where the web is fast running out of addresses. As we switch to a new standard called IPv6 which will be able to support up to 340 trillion trillion trillion web addresses there will be an increasing trend towards creating smart networks of communication of web-connected objects. It is not unfeasible that through their own, store-installed chip the jeans you bought this morning are tweeting your location as you walk across

the park or boogie your way down to your local
nightclub.

The technology, running on tiny radio-frequency
identification devices (RFID) is intended to automate
tasks such as inventory tracking and even supermarket
checkouts but it's finding a home in other uses as well.

One such use is in Toyota hybrid electric cars.
Toyota has always been one of the frontrunners in
linked up technology and now it has decided to team up
with Salesforce.com to allow cars to chat to their drivers
on a private social network.

The venture, called Toyota Friend, will first work
only for hybrid and electric cars. So if the battery is
almost flat, for instance, the driver would receive a short
message via Bluetooth on his or her smartphone alerting
them of the fact and letting them know the time when
the re-charging of the battery would be complete.
Toyota hybrids can also update their location and the
length of time they have spent in each place.

The connection of objects to the web and their
ability to communicate with their owners and each
other, if necessary, is called by industry experts IoT
which is short for Internet of Things. The vision (and it's
truly breathtaking in scope) is to create always-on
networks which are activated by specific stimuli
(motion, body-heat, specific environmental conditions)
and broadcast information using RFID technology.

Imagine a smart building where a manager can
know how many people are inside just by which rooms
are reflecting motion, for instance, via motion-sensitive
lights. This could help save lives in an emergency.

The idea of connectivity in such a scale raises the
possibility that before too long we will live in 'smart'

cities equipped with smart cameras everywhere, detectors and non-invasive neurosensors scanning our brains for overt activity in every street. Advertising and promotion will take place according to the reading of these sensors, looking for full engagement rather than disinterested eyeballs which just need distraction.

Another way to make things smarter is by embedding sensors in them and sending data online via a wireless low-power technology called Zigbee.

IBM is doing just that. Its project remotely monitors the environment that could affect the health of elderly people in Bolzano, Italy, has extended caretaker supervision with sensors embedded all over the patients' homes. The sensors provide round-the-clock peace of mind not only for the patients but for their families too, without the need for more intrusive check-up methods.

The sensors, for instance, read the levels of carbon monoxide, carbon dioxide, methane, temperature and smoke, and send the information to the caretakers' PCs and mobile devices improving their ability to look after their charges.

A Spanish company called Worldsensing, has come up with a similar sensor-based technology and has put it to a different use. With the help of a special app on their smartphone, drivers can receive data from sensors installed in parking spaces, telling them where the closest free spot is. This saves a significant amount of time which would be spent looking for a parking spot. In addition, it cuts down on city traffic congestion, improves fuel efficiency, provides real savings in unused fuel and cuts down on emissions which would be bad for the environment.

It all sounds wonderful, a connected, interconnecting future where devices communicate with us and each other, exclusively for our benefit. But if you happen to have read any of the many articles regarding privacy concerns and how careless Facebook has been with the handling of the personal data of its user base, you have every right to be worried.

If we live in a sea of information where our activities, location, purchase history, likes, dislikes and pretty much everything else we do is monitored, recorded and stored somewhere it stands to reason that we will need an update on the privacy laws to help us control who sees our data and what they do with it, and a way to do so which is easy to understand.

The dark side of so much information sharing and storing is that it could potentially lead to abuses of such scale as to make anything we have seen in the past pale by comparison. At stake will be issues such as personal freedom, human rights and, even, our personal safety.

The upside of all this connectivity is that when it comes to living, working and doing pretty much everything else we may, soon, live in a world where the online and offline worlds are so seamlessly integrated and connected through social (as well as private) networks that we will not actually think of the word 'social' in the context we do today, at all.

Your friends, for instance, may well know where your car has been (because it told them). They may be able to connect with you and arrange a trip (or a stay over) as you go somewhere for business. You may be able to access vital tourist information or motel reviews, when you most need it, because other friends have

198

taken a similar trip before and there is already socialised data readily available regarding parking places, hotels and restaurants and even flight times and (maybe) helpful booking clerks.

Stewart Brand, erstwhile editor of *the Whole Earth Catalog* and digital frontier pioneer, seems to have been right. Information, as he said, does want to be free, and the cost of getting it out is getting lower and lower all the time. However he was also right when he said, in the same sentence that "information wants to be expensive, because it's so valuable. The right information in the right place just changes your life." How we go about reconciling these two tendencies in a way that the information we collect acquires value, has some intrinsic function and provides meaning comes down to the way we set up and use social media not tomorrow, or the near future, but right now.

Swimming in the sea of information we are about to get, the smart money is not in acquiring information, that particular bit is going to be both low-cost and easy, but in classifying it so that it actually means something.

IBM, learnt most of its painful lessons about business in the 90s and, these days, never stands still or blindly believes that advances in technology cannot lay to waste a corporation which has failed to evolve. So it is already busy investing in the acquisition of firms and technologies designed to give it the data mining capability necessary to turn the noise of social media into a meaningful signal which it can then sell at a profit.

## Data mining and social mood

Before social media came along marketers and pollsters had market research companies conduct street interviews, holding clipboards and asking passers-by questions. There were organised focus group tests and paid polls and, surveys and an entire universe of enticements designed to do nothing more than get information which would be indicative of a particular mood, trend, belief or outcome which could then be sold to those who needed it.

Political careers, new products, millions of dollars of potential sales and the fate of the entire advertising industry often hung in the balance, on these and though they were far from perfect, they were the only thing standing between an 'educated guess' (which a mid-level corporate or party exec could take to his superior which he could then use to sell something to the board of directors or party leadership) and the traditional casting of the bones which would point which way the decision making should go.

Social media has provided us with techniques which are far kinder to chickens and a lot more accurate than anything polls, paid or otherwise, could hope to give us.

Imagine a supercomputer which when fed sufficient social media data can predict global unrest, local revolutions and, presumably, market crashes, all before they happen, or even appear imminent. I know this is in the realm of science fiction, a little like UniComp in *This Perfect Day*, Colossus in *Colossus: The Forbin Project* or Skynet in *Terminator*. Yet, Kalev Leetaru, from the University of Illinois' Institute for

Computing in the Humanities, Arts and Social Science did just that. Leetaru used an SGI Altix supercomputer, known as Nautilus, based at the University of Tennessee to which he fed hundreds of millions of articles drawn from the world of news gathering and social media.

The news angle of the articles was required for direction while the social media angle was necessary for what is now called Mood Detection or 'automated sentiment mining', basically an analysis of social media articles, responses and noise for words such as 'terrible', 'horrific' or 'nice' which then determine a rise or dip in sentiment in a given social graph in a specific geographic location.

Working retrospectively and going back to data over a 30 year period Leetaru found that the computer's analysis could precisely predict the Arab Spring happening in Egypt and Tunisia, it predicted, correctly, the revolution in Libya and even suggested the correct location of Bin Laden within 200 km of where he was found and in direct contradiction to the CIA-generated body of analysis which placed him elsewhere.

Leetaru's supercomputer used an algorithm which analysed as many as 100 trillion interconnected relationships around each story, examining the intricate web of social media interaction which sprung up around it and the reactions it created.

Generally speaking, data mining (sometimes called data or knowledge discovery) is the process of analysing data from different perspectives and summarizing it into useful information - information that can then be used to increase revenue, cut costs, or both. The word itself however has become one of social media's buzzwords alongside 'mood mining' which allows us to discover, analyze and then accurately predict sentiment over a particular product or event with a very small margin of error.

This is the new world which social media has made possible and which marketers, advertisers and politicians are only just now taking the first steps to come to grips with.

The principle behind this, which is driving innovation, is a simple one. If we can somehow, analyze the sentiment of the crowd, if we have access to the unguarded thoughts, and feelings which leak out of the online masses through social media interactions, we will have at our disposal a much better crystal ball than we could ever have hoped for.

We will be able, for instance, to pick out stock options which are doing great, before they even start to show their potential just by selecting to analyze the sentiment around a company's brand, which should be a reflection of the feelings of the purchasing crowd of its products.

We will be able to predict blockbuster films and best-selling books by successfully analyzing the 'noise' that's created around them, the mentions they get and the degree of sharing, re-sharing and interaction they generate.

We will be able to craft advertising campaigns which play upon current interests or address specific, trending concerns. Heck, we will even be able to predict political party wins and losses more accurately than exit polls and before the official count comes in.

You begin to understand the importance and power of social media analysis.

202

There are two quick questions to answer here before we jump in and see just how some of this, at least, can be achieved right now, the moment you finish reading this chapter and without a supercomputer.

The first one is how accurate can these predictions be? The second is whether there is a medium bias we need to be aware of.

Obviously, they are both related. When it comes to mining sentiment on the web the predictive tools we have rely on channels such as Twitter where the 140 character limit is itself a factor. For instance, the tight word count of the medium may increase the use of superlatives. In itself this is not a limitation provided the measuring algorithm takes account of this and normalizes it. As we do not control the settings of the tools we use however and it is not always possible to know their sensitivity, this is something which we need to hold firmly in mind, every time we engage in mood mining ourselves.

## Data mining techniques

The web, from the very first instance, did something revolutionary. It allowed the individual to perform to the same level and enjoy the same capabilities as a corporation through the use of refined digital tools.

As a result of this the guy working out of his garage armed with a great idea and the willingness to turn his belief in himself into hard work could give market giants a run for their money, provided he was focused, understood what he was doing and was willing to put in some graft.

This is a trend which has continued in terms of research and analysis to this day. In the past just to get some quality data on a market trend, a product or a service you needed to have, at your fingertips, a team of analysts and some pretty sophisticated software. Right now all you need is the ability to use some free online tools and the time to do it properly.

If you are ready to do your own data mining experiment here are five social media tools to help you do it:

**1. TweetReach** (http://tweetreach.com) – Whenever you use Twitter you wonder just who sees your Tweets, whether they retweet them, respond to them or pass them on. TweetReach enables you to mine Twitter for that data using any search term you desire and gauging the results. The one small restriction is that it limits this to your last 50 Tweets, which seems to be fair in terms of relevancy and in order to reduce noise in the results. Now you never have to wonder if your online marketing is working.

**2. Google Trends** (http://google.com/trends) – Input a search term of your choosing in Google Trends and watch how the search volume for that search terms evolves across time, geographic regions plus what news there has been regarding it. Invaluable when it comes to actually seeing how interest on something peaks or wanes, it is a valuable research and analysis tool.

**3. Google Alerts** (http://google.com/alerts) – Google alerts allows you to mine Google and its vast web indexing resources and be notified the moment something relevant to your interests breaks the surface on the web. Useful as both an early warning and a corroborative research tool, Google Alerts can be used to track the reach of your marketing, alert you to breaking news stories, give you an indication of whether interest in a trend is peaking and keep you abreast of the wave in terms of information.

**4. The US Government's Open Source Centre** (https://www.opensource.gov/public/content/login/login.fcc) – By their own words: "The Open Source Center (OSC) is the US Government's premier provider of foreign open source intelligence. OpenSource.gov provides information on foreign political, military, economic, and technical issues beyond the usual media to an ever expanding universe of open sources." This means that when you want to be ahead of the wave in knowledge of what's hot across the web the Open Source Centre can do all of the hard work for you.

**5. Monitoring the BBC news gathering service** (http://www.monitor.bbc.co.uk/) – The *Monitoring BBC* service is another free media monitoring service which summarises stories breaking across all of the BBC's significant news gathering presence. This way it has the ability to show not just what's breaking across the globe on almost any front (politics, environment, consumer issues, economy and tech) but also to provide a concise view of interest and responses as they develop.

Taken together all these five tools give every webmaster, marketer and researcher the ability to second-guess trends with greater accuracy than ever before. This means that you could now put in place online marketing campaigns which ride on the coat-tails of breaking news stories or social media trends and utilise the web in a way which creates greater interaction and engagement at a lower cost and with greater efficiency.

## Social media drives everything

In this chapter we saw how social media has risen to become one of the motive forces driving the development of interaction on the web and the creation of more open, more precisely targeted communications off it.

Like a magic ingredient introduced into a broth of already exotic tastes, social media is a catalyst which is changing everything beyond the narrow sphere of variables we can hope to control.

Its effects are incremental but they are cumulative and they are, slowly but inevitably, leading to better advertising, better films, better books, better ways to communicate. All of these, taken collectively point to a picture where the web is no longer just changing, it is now changing us. It is changing the way we do things. It is changing the way we operate in our businesses, it is changing our marketing techniques and it is changing the way we think.

It is upon the last of these that we shall focus now.

# ■Chapter 11
## The Future of the Social Web

Social networks are poised to take over the web. Facebook has 800 million active users (more than 10% of the planet's population), Twitter produces over a billion tweets a week, Google+ is growing at a phenomenal level which may, by the end of 2012, see it become the second major player, in terms of numbers, behind Facebook. LinkedIn has just passed the 100 million sign ups.

The expectation is that soon enough there will be social commerce, social search, social deals, social viewing and a 'new' social economy based upon all this. Right now, some of these have actually been put into practice (like social search) but the rest are a mixture of buzzwords of the moment and hope (what exactly is social commerce and how will it differ from our currently used ecommerce?).

Quibbles aside however, make no mistake, 'Social' is indeed changing everything and, as social networks continue to grow the social ingredient (if we can call it that) is, ultimately, shaping the web we will have and much of the way we will interact when online. The reason for this is time.

When you are online you are using up time which has been taken from some other aspect of your life. Already in the US and in the UK people are watching less TV than ever before and they are using the time they free up through reduced TV viewing, to be online, longer. When you have only so many hours in the day and only so much time to spend online, the web is defined by where you choose to spend it.

Businesses and marketers strongly believe in the principle of "fishing where the fish are" which, in practice, means that the bulk of services, offers, deals and information, along with the functionality underpinning it all, inevitably begins to shift, relocating where the social networks are. Within that relocating trend there would be preferences, guided by the need for efficiency, which would favour the dominant social networks.

Right now this means Facebook, Google+ and Twitter. While the social network landscape may change the practice of gravitating towards dominant social networks for businesses and individuals, is unlikely to.

It was Facebook's founder, Zuckerberg, who popularized the term 'social graph' at the Facebook f8 conference on May 24, 2007, when he used it to explain that the Facebook Platform, which was introduced at the same time, would benefit from the social graph by taking advantage of the relationships between individuals, that Facebook provides, to offer a richer online experience.

Because our time online has become precious we have all become incredibly adept at protecting it.

208

Without even realising it we act as the critics upon whose opinion website design and refinements in search are based. Websites which take a little longer to load (and we are talking about seconds rather than minutes) are clicked away from impatiently and never revisited. Websites which serve us pop ups asking us to sign up to something the moment we land on their homepage, are clicked away from in irritation. Changes in Google search which autofill our typing as we type the search query, get our vote and save us, cumulatively, minutes each day.

The tendency to be impatient, to want things to be instant and the desire to safeguard the quality of our online experience is what is powering developments of the social graph on most social networks with the lead role in this, right now, taken by Facebook.

This is not as rosy as it may sound. As you might suspect the very things which help us online, when they are used unchecked, can also create deep issues which could potentially harm us.

## The social graph and the interest graph

As individuals we are all very complicated. We are interested in things which lie outside our expertise and which may not be of immediate practical use to us. Quantum physicists could collect match boxes, for instance, and matchbox makers could follow quantum physics. Hard-nosed marketers may follow romantic fiction and romantic fiction novelists may market like pros.

The point is that, as human beings, we resist being pigeonholed and what defines us is not the social graph, which can loosely be defined as "This is who I know" but our interest graph which is more closely aligned to the notion of "this is what I like".

The distinction is a significant one. In Google+ I may have in my circles Sasha Grey (a former porn star turned mainstream actress) and Summer Daniels (an author of intelligent erotica) but the reasons for that lie more in what I am interested in the psychological dynamics governing their career choices than their professions.

Should the information about me centre around my social graph then, on paper, I would be a prime candidate for every marketer of porn and erotic fiction, areas which I have not spent any money on since I was eighteen.

At the Facebook f8 conference in September 2011 Zuckerberg announced a new 'frictionless' sharing which went a step beyond the better-known 'Facebook Connect' which asks you to use your Facebook login in order to join a particular website so you can comment on its content or access its services.

Zuckerberg's vision of frictionless sharing is intended to remove the number of steps necessary in order to share something with your Facebook friends, so, the moment you go on a website and login using your Facebook account your friends can see where you were, what you looked at and what you did while there.

This automatic sharing of your activity is powered by the social graph. Its development has been brought about by a real market need and the sense of something lacking.

Before The Facebook f8 September conference of 2011 there was much navel-watching amongst internet marketers looking to discover why social marketing was not working.

Companies were implementing their advice. They were creating Facebook pages and they were driving eyeballs to them, they were creating Twitter accounts and they were Tweeting away through them and yet the line of proof leading from these actions to the respective companies' bottom lines was harder to find than salmon trails in frothy water.

Clearly something was wrong and the 'wrong' lay in the fact that almost everybody was falling in the trap of mistaking the social graph for the interest graph. Companies whose Facebook pages had 50,000+ fans were not getting the kind of attention which would lead to sales because they happened to have the wrong 50,000+ fans.

This same story was (and is) being enacted across many boardrooms and sales conferences where 'social' continues to mean a channel rather than a mind-set.

The issue has never been more clearly outlined than in a 2011 study which showed that UK consumers interact very little with brands. The study, conducted by TNS, one of the largest custom research specialists in the world, showed that after analysing results involving 72,000 consumers in 60 countries it found that nearly two thirds of UK consumers do not want to engage with brands on social media.

For those of us who have been looking at social media through rosy coloured glasses and seeing a massive, global playground where a brand would post a marketing message which would then be instantly picked up by those playing there and shared round their friends, this was nothing less than a dousing with 100 gallons of icy-cold water.

What? Why? How? Were the gasps being heard amongst company marketers following the publication of the study. Was not social media supposed to provide the means for the ultimate connection? Well, actually no. Social media is not a corporate channel. It is not even a communication channel as such. As a matter of fact it is not even a channel.

Social media is an environment and as such it has the same limitations as offline advertising. The adverts which work best offline are the ones which tell a story. They are the ones which pique the interest of their audience who find in them just the right mix between entertainment, information and a sales message.

I am not sure, here, which is worse. The fact that we are making all these basic mistakes, as marketers, in social media or the fact that every time a new medium comes along we throw away all forms of common sense and leap in with both feet expecting it to provide the answer to our prayers and deliver instant rewards for practically no effort involved, at all?

If you are a marketer and you are reading this, then you must know that everything you know and everything you have learnt is relevant in social media. You also need to know that as a new means of communication social media has tropes and rules you need to discover which means you have to be willing to experiment in order to understand what works and what doesn't.

# Social media guidelines

The rules of engagement in a social media environment are simple enough. To understand them we will need to revisit the results of a study rather unsexily labelled: *Following the Crowd: Brain Substrates of Long Term Memory Conformity* where neuroscientists, Micah Edelson, Tali Sharot, Raymond Dolan and Yadin Dudai, conducted research which showed that volunteers who watched a short film and three days later answered a questionnaire about what they had seen in order to test their recollection of the events of the film, could, generally, be both accurate and truthful about it.

Four days later the volunteers were asked back in and given more questions about the film while hooked up to a brain scanner. This time, they were provided with an additional memory jogger in the form of replies to similar questions provided by the other members of the group.

Although the volunteers did not know it the answers on the memory jogger had been fabricated and bore no relation to the real answers given by the other members of the group. The results this time were remarkable: 70 per cent of those who had the memory jogger changed their own answers to fit what they perceived was the group norm departing from their original recollection of the film's events, of just four days prior.

This immediately demonstrates two things every school kid who wants to survive already knows: first that to deviate from the group norm is undesirable and second to stray from the pack makes for a lonely experience. To further test their hypothesis the researchers now called the volunteers back and revealed to them that the memory jogger had contained false answers. Wiring them up again to the brain scanner they repeated the battery of questions about the events in the short film they'd seen. While some volunteers went back to their earlier version of events, almost half persisted with the false answers of their previous session.

## How social media marketing really works

As human beings we are hardwired to be social animals. We also are natural storytellers. Our brains are actively involved in editing our memories of the world around us and the people we interact with. This is both a means of gaining acceptance within a social group and a defence mechanism which helps us establish, at a personal level, a sense of hierarchy and identity within it.

We are, in other words, constantly engaged in a dialogue in our heads which edits, changes and, arguably, augments the memories we have, discarding details which do not fit in with the accepted storyline we want to have so as to better fit in our 'story' to our perceived version of the world.

The fishing trip we went on last summer ends up, in the retelling, being akin to a whale hunt worthy of Captain Ahab. The golf course shot we took is stretched by 300 yards and the cost of the birthday bash we threw can now pay off the sovereign debt of Ireland and maybe Spain.

The researchers' fMRI data proved useful by allowing the comparison of the differences in brain activity between the last questioning, where those who were asked gave a persistently false version of events, and the one before where they were perhaps knowingly lying in order to fit in with social norm (the so called peer-group pressure effect). If changes were noted then it would provide concrete proof that not only are we capable of lying socially but that we can alter our physical recollection of the truth so that our brain can no longer distinguish between the lie and what really happened.

The study revealed strong co-activation between the hippocampus and the amygdala in the brain. The hippocampus is long known to play a role in the way long-term memory is stored in the brain , while the amygdala controls emotions in the brain. According to the scientists, the co-activation of these areas can sometimes result in the replacement of an accurate memory with a false one, provided the false memory has a social component. This suggests that the feedback of others has the ability to strongly shape our remembered experience to the point that we can, shockingly, fabricate a 'truth'.

The findings suggest a number of things which we have been looking at in connection with social media marketing from a layman's perspective already:

▸ **Narrative drive.** It has been mentioned countless times to let your social media marketing 'tell a story'. We see now that marketing which has the capacity to become part of a wider narrative has also the greatest potential to be remembered, disseminated, talked about and, ultimately, succeed in persuading people to make a purchase. Similarly, if you are starting something new you should expect to have to do a lot of hard work before you even begin to see any hint of results.

‣ **Consistency.** Change your 'story' or message too many times, or create narrative drives which are too fragmented to be understood and you are seriously weakening the effectiveness of your marketing.

‣ **Critical mass.** Obviously, the more people talk about your brand or message the greater the chance there is of it becoming part of the narrative of others and thus helping you gain brand awareness, market penetration and more sales. Notice that here you need an actively engaged critical mass so the study supports the need for engagement in your social media audience. Having a lot of inert (non-active) followers, would produce no result.

‣ **Influence.** Opinions clearly matter as does influence and the peddling of it. No one, now, can ever again ignore a single negative Tweet, criticising post or simply ride roughshod over online complaints. All of these, however, provide an excellent opportunity for deeper interaction and to help further reinforce the narrative drive you are creating.

‣ **Peer group pressure.** Although I doubt if anyone would ever own up to buying something simply because their friends have it, the study makes it abundantly clear that subconsciously we are hardwired to try and fit in. Great news for Ford then, not so good for the upcoming DeLorean with the new electric motor.

‣ **Attention to detail.** The brain is a powerful filter. It can create patchwork narratives, choosing which bits to ignore and which to keep, provided there is some kind of overall cohesion which confers a benefit

216

for the individual. After all, no one wants to weave a narrative for their social group which will make them look lame to their peers. This means that there has to be a clear strategy to all social media marketing with precise aims, feedback mechanisms and tweaking along the way.

If narrative drive and engagement play such a strong part in social media, it goes to reason, that so does charisma. After all, before we are wrapped in the 'story' we really want to know who the storyteller is.

The late Steve Jobs made great use of his charisma at Apple conferences, standing in for the personification of the 'cool' that was his company's products.

Richard Branson became the face of Virgin standing, in consumers' minds, for approachability, familiarity, a hint of entertainment and a reversal of the status quo, even when he was anything but.

Zuckerberg has taken a leaf out of Jobs' playbook and has become the face of the company he founded.

These are the successes. Mike Lazaridis, founder and co-CEO of RIM which owns the Blackberry brand, would have been served better had he made a spokesperson issue the public apology he posted on YouTube about the Blackberry outage during four days in October 2011. Not only did his apology did not work but his own resentment at having to make it was so palpable that Blackberry found itself saddled with even more negative publicity afterwards and nationwide lawsuits for breach of its service contract in the US and Canada.

Of course if you happen to be in the hot seat and you have not got charisma (and you know it) what do you do?

The classic answer here is you turn the problem on its head and make a virtue out of a necessity. No one would have batted an eyelid, for instance, has Lazaridis publicly stated that he hates having to make his public apology (it was obvious anyway) and that he hates both the time it is taking and the focus it is drawing away from more pressing issues which require his attention. And, had he then gone on and explained that his attention on those pressing issues is what makes Blackberry products great and that his focus is on problems like the outage not happening ever again, he would have won a massive PR victory.

What Steve Jobs and Richard Branson cultivated so seemingly effortlessly, now has to become the norm rather than the exception.

The TNS study really did not reveal that UK consumers hate being marketed to by brands in social networks, it really revealed that UK consumers hate being marketed to by faceless, corporate brands in social networks.

Like door-to-door salesmen in the offline world brand advertising in social media settings is seen as an intrusion of their environment by someone intended to sell them something. The marketing message itself nothing more than the salesman's shoe jammed in the doorway.

So, to avoid creating these impressions in social media marketing strive to create authenticity. Tell a story. Be engaging. Above all entertain. Be light in how you communicate and think that what you really want

218

to do is for those who will become your customers and those who are your customers, to get to know you better and you to get to know them better.

Because social media changes everything, we need to learn to change with it. Anything else is doomed to failure, as the TNS study so clearly demonstrated.

# ■Chapter 12
## Authenticity and the Social Web

My grandfather used to know a lot of people. Anyone he did not like however (and as he got older the list grew longer) was immediately labelled as 'fake'. I was just a kid at the time so I do not know exactly what he understood by that, nor why he put so much store by authenticity, but as I witnessed him, on more than one occasion, muttering under his breath at the retreating back of someone he had just held a long conversation with: "fake", it was impressed upon me that being 'real' was something to really aspire to.

I often wonder, had he been alive today (he passed away before the end of the last century) what he would have made of social media and the Facebook generation.

To him the greatest insult he could level at anyone was to say that they were not real. He lived through the second world war and even fought in the Balkans, sometime before that so identity and a sense of being real, was important to him.

220

On the web it has become easier to re-invent anything and anyone. As a result 'authenticity' has become the new currency. Being able to feel comfortable in the knowledge of who we are dealing with or at least have a sense that we know the core values of the entity we are dealing with, is what this is all about.

I say 'entity' instead of person because the need to understand who we connect with online and what they represent now also encompasses businesses and brands and this is where the real million dollar question is being asked: How does a business or a brand become 'open' in social media? Surely, the brand is an asset of the business, as closely guarded as secret recipes and strategic marketing plans, to throw it wide open to the public at large seems madness at best, suicidal at its worst.

In October 2010, as the recession showed few signs of abetting, GAP, the iconic clothes retailer, decided that what was needed to help pull its stores out of the doldrums and revitalize sales was a new logo which would reflect the brand's ever evolving identity.

To those of us watching with interest the trajectory of traditional retailers and big name brands in the social media age it was not a surprising move. As early as 2007, GAP's creative director, Patrick Robinson, had revealed his interest in keeping GAP modern and fresh as part of his plan to "elevate the brand."

What happened next is obvious only in retrospect. The moment the new GAP logo appeared there was a strong negative reaction from all the GAP fans. More than that, beyond the thousands of tweets and Facebook status updates deriding its design, people found other creative ways to protest the new logo, like creating very bad versions of their own and sharing them online. A fake Twitter account gathered thousands of followers, and GAP logo generators quickly went viral.

The pressure was so intense that within five days of unveiling its new logo GAP had officially reversed its decision and reverted to the old logo its fans loved.

It was the first major case of a social media backlash becoming a reason for a corporate U-turn. It also marked the moment when the realisation happened: in the social media age your brand is no longer yours. If you are successful, it now belongs to the people who believe in you and what you stand for and these people, rightly or wrongly, now have a stake in it. If the brand belongs to them and they feel passionately about it, it stands to reason that if you are now going to 'mess' with it and change it you'd better make sure that there is a complete information and consultation process in place, making it feel like it is truly a joint decision. Fail in that and you will feel what GAP felt when its name became, practically overnight, a social media joke.

## Openness should be your social media strategy

If you are serious about making inroads in the social media age you need to create an online presence which is as interesting, transparent, engaging and entertaining as if we just met at a party and you were wired to a lie detector.

This means that the traditional approach of a marketing department which did its 'thing' and maybe a PR person who would do their 'thing' when some of the 'things' the marketing department did backfired and needed fixing, will no longer work.

We spent the closing years of the last century and the first five or so years of this one living in the time of spin and the age of spin doctors. The feeling was that no matter what the news was, there was always a way to manage it using the best of technology and mass media so that what lasting impression remained was what you wanted to remain.

As a result we found ourselves drawn into two wars in Iraq and Afghanistan which possibly could have been avoided and certainly should have been handled better, and a global credit crunch which no one is 100% sure how it came about but which everyone feels is someone else's fault.

Now, I know that the global credit crunch was not the result of spin and even the Iraq war might still have happened given the popular sentiment at the time, but both these events are indicative of the fallout which happens when the only consistency you achieve in public communication is one of subterfuge and, sometimes, outright lies.

Values then lose out to expediency, the end always justifies the means and the world begins to assume a look reminiscent of a looking glass world where there are consecutive layers of dissemblance covering an ever shrinking kernel of truth.

Apply that in business and the odds are that sooner or later you will crash and burn, your fatal stumble brought about by the simplest of events.

The naïve will always believe that truth and openness bulletproofs you. It doesn't. But if we take the logical point of view that you will always have to react to adversity and take measures to meet it, then it becomes easier when all you have to do is focus on dealing with the problem at hand and surviving, rather than worrying about how you are going to cover up mistakes, faults and falsehoods.

This is where what I call, for lack of a better term, Truth Marketing, comes in. There is a perception in business, born out of real cases, that marketing and advertising are there to lie. There is a pseudo-scientific basis to this approach which has been fuelled by countless studies which show that purchasing decisions are emotional rather than rational.

Over the years this has led to a kind of lopsided corporate thinking which goes a little like this: Provided that the product or service being sold is of real value consumers are incapable of making any decisions based on facts which means that in order for them to decide to access a service or buy a product they need to be told exactly what they want to hear about it rather than the truth itself.

For much of the 20th century adverts presented a picture of services and products which did not quite match their reality. Marketing back then was all about the hype, relying for success on what I call the 'cattle herd response' where the moment something reaches critical mass it becomes instantly desirable irrespective of its real merits. Do three million people own a yellow umbrella? The ubiquitous nature of the product and the fact that it has been purchased so many times would give it instant credibility. There was no question whether a yellow umbrella is better than a black one when it comes to looking good or keeping you dry from the rain. It simply had to be bought.

Hype, however, while it may deliver some success and it may indeed kick-start a 'cattle herd response' will only get you so far. This, in the past, led to inevitable fads whereby some kind of sense kicked in at a later date or the product finally lost its lustre as the cold, hard truth of its ordinariness finally seeped in or, even more simply, it was replaced by the 'next hot thing' to hit the advertising and marketing horizons.

In some ways nothing has changed. As consumers we are still inundated by adverts and hype and a lot of effort, ingenuity and money goes into creating the next fad, simply because there is a lot of money to be made in this. Some things however are different.

What has changed in the marketing and advertising horizons?

Well, if you are part of a large company the first sign that things are different will lie in the fact that your return-on-investment (ROI) analysis will have been showing, for the last ten years, a diminishing return for your advertising buck. Simply put, in the 21st century you get a lot less in sales for the amount of money you spend in traditional advertising and marketing.

If you are running your own bootstrap business where you end up wearing most of the hats you will have noticed the same thing in a different way: you need to spend more and more cash just to make an impact in a marketplace that is teeming with competitors, a marketplace where consumer attention is now being distracted by millions of voices.

Both perspectives beg the same question: what should be done to actually get a more positive result in sales? The answer to both the corporate exec struggling

to find a solution and the lone internet entrepreneur
looking to make his online business standout is the
same: tell the truth. This is not as radical as it sounds,
still, I know I need to explain it further.

In order for truth marketing to work for you
there are a few assumptions we must make which really
should be a given in any business:

‣ **First** – your business model has to be rock solid.
You need to have a clear idea of what you are selling,
how and to whom.

‣ **Second** – the quality of what you are selling is
commoditized. That means that you have reached, at
the very least, the minimum acceptable standard and
have improved on it and you never drop below that
mark (though you should always find ways to rise
above it).

‣ **Third** – There is a real need for what you are
selling. This has to be true even if the product is so new
that it does not yet have a clear-cut market. If there is no
real need for your product then you really are sunk
before you've even got started.

‣ **Fourth** – You have a clear development strategy
for your business. Even the best product in the world
has a finite lifecycle which is modelled on the Bell
Curve of diminishing demand. If there is no model
available to take your company forward through
innovation or the introduction of new products you will
then be doomed to fail even if you have done everything
right.

Provided these four are in place then closing the
gap between you and your potential audience requires a
step whereby you tell the truth about what you are
doing or what your product does and why. Contrary to

popular belief consumers are not idiots. Nor are they 'cattle'. And in the 21st century the cottage-industry empowerment granted by the web and the ability to work online has created a new class of consumer.

The person you are targeting today is aware of the effort and energy which goes into bringing a product to the market. They are also aware of and resistant, to hype. They understand the need to market and they are looking for information which is engaging, non-condescending and actually gives them everything they need in order to make an honest, informed decision.

This does not mean that you cannot or should not use hype in your marketing in order to create an entertaining experience. The Old Spice Man adverts featuring Isaiah Mustafa's brawny torso, after all, are pure entertaining hype created to bring focus back to a brand that had almost reached its sell-by date.

I have used the Old Spice advert as an example on purpose. It has been a wildly successful viral video campaign for P & G, it won awards, it became the talking point for millions of online viewers, it changed the purchasing habits of female consumers and it increased the sales of Old Spice. It also highlighted the fact that in the 21st century you really need to engage your customers in a partnership which allows them to invest themselves in your product and its marketing.

The Old Spice adverts achieved exactly that. The quality of the product was always beyond question. What it lacked was street cred and the adverts supplied that in spades. This brings us to the question of what consumers really want.

This has never been an easy question to answer. Pre-21st century we had to rely on market research and the informal polls taken by the sales department to give us an inkling of what they want. Today the web itself gives us much of the valuable data we have in hand.

The GAP logo fiasco and the similar case surrounding the change of the Starbucks logo show that there is a powerful paradigm shift which has taken place in the 21st century which can no longer be ignored. Consumers now are an integral part of a brand's and a product's life cycle and development. In other words the customers you most want to attract need to not be marketed to, rather than marketed at, with a view to recruiting them as brand and product advocates.

Believe it or not consumers want to believe in the products they buy. After all they invest in them heavily themselves through money, emotional investment (the purchasing response) and the image they project through its use. What they need is a product (or brand) which actually allows this degree of participation and makes them feel proud, valued members of its family.

For companies used to micro-managing everything from the font size of the text which goes in their print ads to the way their product are shown this takes a huge leap of faith and a handing over of control from its marketing and PR departments to its customers.

Small businesses have less to lose (they have smaller ad budgets for a start), they are likely to be a lot less controlling at any rate and for them the opportunity to tap into viral marketing is more attractive than the risk that it may rebound on them. You will, quite rightly, ask me here, 'ok, say I take this leap of faith and hand control of my product over to my customers, what do I stand to gain and what do I stand to lose?'

Truth marketing is a conceptual leap. If you have a small business and met me down at your local watering hole I have little doubt that in less than a minute you would have been able to convince me to become your customer. This is because, at a personal level with one-to-one contact you would be engaging, honest, possibly witty and certainly would have been interested in me becoming your customer to our mutual benefit.

On paper every company marketing today wants the same thing. However in the transition from aim to practice, marketing lore intercedes and something is always lost in translation. Truth marketing is about getting that 'lost' element back. How? The answer is actually simpler than you may think.

What usually happens when a product goes live and its marketing begins is that the marketing department does not talk to sales and sales never really get much involved with marketing. Incredibly enough I have seen the same pride in a one-man outfit where the marketing message seemed to have absolutely nothing to do with the sales info. Whether this was a case of an individual who simply managed to wear different hats with a 100% success or a perfect example of the pride between marketing and sales as an action, I was not really able to determine, but it did serve to highlight the issue for me.

So start off with a piece of paper and simply list what your product does, the approach can work for a service also. List what it does better, what it does worse (and why) and why it is different from everyone else's (or if it isn't then at least list why it would make sense to buy it from you and not any of your competitors).

The moment you have all this in front of you, you also have your truth marketing formula. Yes, you can then dress it up with whimsy, wit, imagery or anything else you like. You can chunk it up and parse it out in a dozen informational ads, if you so wish. In its entirety though what you do should always be subject to what your product is and what it does and why you are the perfect choice to buy it from.

One perfect example of Truth Marketing was the original Goodyear tires advert which marketed their tires as 'all-weather tires'. Many saw this as simply clever sloganeering but in essence this was an early, and very successful, form of Truth Marketing. Goodyear tires were all-weather. Of course, all tires are all-weather, but Goodyear was the first company to stress this for their own tires and managed to get the phrase associated with them as a result.

Truth Marketing works because it appeals to consumers' common sense and, as such, usually presents a winning proposition which under scrutiny only gets stronger. It works even when applied in a traditional, controlling, top-down method of communication. It certainly works when you grasp the courage of your own convictions and throw the reputation of what you sell at the mercy of the social network crowd. Scary? You bet! But the rewards, as we shall see, are enormous. Let's take a look at them:

> ‣ **Viral marketing** – engage your customers fully and, like the Old Spice advert, you will get a loyal, unpaid, marketing force eager to spread the good news about your brand.

› **Market penetration** – explain why buying from you makes sense and you have established an irrefutable selling point which will help you gain more customers.

› **Brand quality** – your products and brand name will be associated, in the minds of those who purchase from you, with a sense of lasting value and quality.

› **Increased sales** – this is always the Holy Grail of marketing. With Truth Marketing you generate a higher word-of-mouth buzz which leads to higher sales.

Like any kind of marketing Truth Marketing also has its pitfalls. Because it relies on giving control of your marketing over to your customers you are never sure just how well it may be working for you. By the time you see problems the chances are that some damage will have been done, which you will then need to work hard to overcome.

The other issue with Truth Marketing you need to be aware of is that it leaves you little room for 'adjustment'. Things are what they are, if a product really does not appeal you have no room to change its image or alter its marketing message without appearing to do the opposite of what Truth Marketing really is, unless of course you really change the product itself.

## Two case studies where Truth Marketing and Openness in social media really work

No look at openness as a social media marketing model would be complete with at least two classic examples.

The first one is Pardot, a marketing automation company that offers its software as a cloud service, often used in conjunction with customer relationship management systems such as SugarCRM. In April 2011, one of the company's co-founders, Adam Blitzer went to the SugarCon conference and talked about a different kind of openness.

In a keynote speech, he talked about how being open about your pricing, and even the dirty laundry of customer complaints about your products, can work as a social media marketing strategy. "There are a lot of things you can really make open and turn to your advantage. Buying has changed so much, with the prospect doing so much more work up front," Blitzer said, and if you frustrate them in their online research, for example, by being coy about your pricing, you're likely to lose them.

Blitzer proposed a clever strategy which he successfully used in the marketing of his company: monitor everything being said about you and respond to it because it achieves three crucial things:

‣ **It creates conversation** (a vital aspect of social media). It allows those who love you and those who hate you to realise that you are actually listening and that you are responding with much more than just canned responses.

‣ **It creates engagement.** Successfully reply to the issue at hand, even if it is a complaint. Do this and you end up with someone who has found out something about your company and its character which they could easily share with those they are engaged with, to your benefit

‣ **It generates vital keywords.** This is perhaps the small stroke of genius Blitzer had. As I have already explained, social media is important precisely because of its impact upon SEO. It is difficult (and maybe even counter-productive) to try and optimize your website or product for negative keywords. Respond to customer complaints adequately however and you are creating a true-value proposition, where those keywords can now show up in search and drive traffic to your company because you are actually being seen to respond.

Blitzer used a small app called Socialite (http://www.apparentsoft.com/socialite) to help keep track of mentions of the company name and his company is small enough for him to be able to train a team so that they know just how to respond (incidentally, this is something basic which RIM, the Blackberry brand owner seemed incapable of doing).

The result is that this activity drives targeted leads to the company's website which can then be turned into customers.

Pardot is a technology company marketing at the cutting edge of its business. It is small, focused and very hungry. I picked it as an example because its use of social media is outstanding even amongst technology companies, but you could argue that they stand a better chance than most of 'getting' social media and using it to their advantage.

So here's the second example. Domino's Pizza. For an everyday pizza company with an OK product which could stand some improvement and competition from practically every quarter (from the supermarket with its frozen, "Authentic Italian Pizza" experience offers, to every local pizzeria which opens up) Domino's Pizza has to rely upon brand recognition and brand power to make that immediate connection with its public which it needs to drive up sales.

What is interesting for Domino's Pizza is that they have achieved this through a two-pronged initiative which follows public sentiment about the company and its products (both the good and the bad) and responds to it and takes that public sentiment on board to help improve its products.

They do this through an app based on their brand, called Pizza Tracker. What makes Domino's Pizza special is that they 'got' social media by being badly burnt.

In April 2009, two employees working for a Domino's Pizza franchise in Conover, N.C., filmed themselves preparing sandwiches and pizza with the food being handled in unsanitary ways (the cheese from the sandwich was rolled up and placed inside the nose of the one of them prior to being put in the sandwich) and posted the tube online on YouTube.

The video was a prank, the food was never delivered. It garnered however more than a million views in just 24 hours, fired up Twitter and got the blogosphere talking about Domino's Pizza in less than savoury ways. More than that, references to the video (which has been taken down by those who posted it for copyright reasons) delivered five out of the ten first page results on Google for the search query 'Domino's Pizza'.

While the company took disciplinary action, polls showed that overnight its image had been badly tarnished with loyal, long-term customers of over 10 years' standing re-thinking their relationship with it.

Worse yet, while it was taking action, putting new processes in place and determining that the two employees (who, incidentally were charged with distributing prohibited foods, the same North Carolina statute that forbids any tampering with Halloween

234

candy) had actually never delivered the food, their apparent silence in social media channels was only fuelling speculation and prolonging the debate.

Domino's were, up to that point, responding like any traditional corporate company has been taught to do. They took action, dealt with the problem and were now hoping that they could stay quiet and it would go away.

Social media does not work like that. By providing a platform where public conversation about your company and brand can take place and anyone can contribute to it, it lays down the challenge for you to participate. Fail to pick it up and you are basically surrendering that conversation to those who are probably least qualified to lead it.

To their credit Domino's Pizza executives learnt fast. Within a day they had established a Twitter account to address the issue (@dpzinfo) and its chief executive had gone on YouTube with a public apology which minced no words.

With this kind of introduction to social media and its power you understand that Domino's Pizza is a company which has learnt the hard way to lead the social media conversation.

As a response to their very public social media crisis Domino's Pizza started to actively collect customer feedback. These reviews weren't kind. As a response, Domino's introduced a new publicly documented initiative which featured all that, called the *Pizza Turnaround* (http://www.pizzaturnaround.com/). The documentary openly shares this negative feedback. Domino's showed clips of customers saying the pizzas tasted like cardboard and were worse than microwaved pizzas. It concluded the documentary with the promise that it would change its ways by improving its recipes, services and products.

The campaign worked. When the approach was first introduced, Domino's had a sales rise of 14% and its stock value doubled.

In July 2011 Domino's Pizza introduced yet one more innovation in social media tracking, their Pizza Tracker is no small-app effort. It invites customers to share their feedback. Their responses can easily be followed at Domino's Twitter account, negative responses included. But the company doesn't stop there: it also directs this feedback live to digital billboards at Times Square, six-foot high pictures, even the less charming ones, are included for a totally authentic experience which makes it impossible to refute the fact that the company is listening.

The company's very public forum sends a clear message to everyone equally: "We may not get things right all the time but we strive to do so all the time."

It is this kind of message which creates trust which, in turn, leads to identification with a brand (and its personality), which can then lead to higher sales.

## The ROI of social media
A chapter which began with authenticity on the web should, rightly, conclude with a few hard examples of how you measure return on your investment (ROI) in social media.

The question of course is a little oxymoronic. Why would 'social media' be any different to the way you measure ROI in, let's say advertising, or an email campaign or a leaflet drop?

Over the past year I have seen more than a dozen separate surveys citing complaints that it is difficult for companies to see a return for their investment in social media and the moment I read that I know that these are companies which are active though social media channels only because their competitors are. It's the familiar territory of my favourite IBM ad of all time where the brochure "doesn't say" why a business should be on the internet though it mentions that the future of business *is* on the internet.

If you want to measure the return of your investment in social media you need to do two basic things: first realise that social media is a journey not a destination. Second, set clear goals for what you want to achieve for your business.

If you are not getting results and you are actually working your social media campaign as you should, the fault lies in what you are doing and how you do it rather than the inability of social media to provide it. Change that, get it right, and the rest should follow.

# Final word

A s authors we usually feel we've achieved the most success in a book when the book itself has become greater than us and better than we envisioned. The idea for *The Social Media Mind* sprang from a number of talks on social media I presented over October and November 2010 where highly-paid executives had leave to attend and ask questions at a level which did not reflect their pay grade.

I originally intended the book to be practical. It takes a long time to read a non-fiction book and even longer to write one and it is always, in my view, better when that time is spent productively, learning something which is of practical value which you can apply to your business, talk about with your colleagues, or use to make more money or get a better job.

The writing process however is not always a tightly controlled one. Books, often, have a habit of taking a mind of their own and dictating what it is they want to contain in their pages. The truth is that social media is not just a marketing concept, although it is true that it is being used as such and throughout this book I have sprinkled a lot of practical things you can do to help shape your social media marketing. Social media is a true change in the way we connect online. Its ability to give voice to the individual is as scary as it is century-defining. I find that it finally brings to life the promise of the web to act as the great leveller, to provide transparency, accountability and a better way not just of working, but living and learning and creating and doing just about anything which involves the word 'social' which, usually, tends to be most things.

This is something which is as exciting as it is frightening to behold and it is this mix of excitement, tinged with fear, that powered many of the detours I took in writing this book. For those detours I apologise.

As I was writing the book the ground kept shifting under my feet. Russia, a country marked by its political apathy, where things have changed in the past thirty years in name only, got social media fever and looked like it was starting its own version of the Arab Spring. Companies ranging from the Bank of America to Verizon were backtracking in service fees intending to do little more than gouge customers some more for what, in the past, used to be free.

GoDaddy, the Texas based, web hosting and domain name registration company found itself in hot water over its support of SOPA and was forced to first retract that support and then, after a strong social media backlash which cost it the loss of 20,000 hosting accounts in a day, publicly announce its opposition to the act.

None of this would have been possible without the ability to spontaneously organise and find like-minded voices which social media provides.

Is the web a cloud based service? Are cloud based services going to hyper-extend the use of social media? Are we heading towards a future where our collective unconscious resides in the cloud and it's accessible through wearable connections or, even, personal augmentations, turning us into cyborgs?

These are questions which pop up all the time at the moment. The socialisation of the web has created a quickening, a true shrinking of the planet and its timezones and a dilution of national boundaries.

Social media, I believe, is an ideal. An idea, if you like which, as ideas often do, means something a little different to each one who comes across it.

A book of ideas and a book of knowledge which can be put into practice, of course, should not be mutually exclusive of each other. It is a comment, perhaps, on the state of the publishing industry that they often are.

Ideas are meant to make you think, even if you reject them. They are there to fire you up, make you analyse for yourself the facts which have led to them and, frequently, even when you agree, the moment they are adopted they lose their proprietary nature and somehow become your own. At that point they are capable of being modified, adapting, mutating, if you will, into whatever new thoughtform the situation calls for.

Knowledge is harder to adapt. It tends to be more hard-edged and precise by necessity. Its existence calls for action more than reflection. The moment you know something and how to do it, you need to put it into practice, sitting on your hands then feels like a total waste of time.

Typically, I write books that fall into one category or the other. This one then is an exception and it was as scary to write as it was exciting. Authors are afraid of showing themselves and they are afraid of being judged in anything other than their work. This is why a book of facts, a practical book of things to do, backed by solid knowledge which is easy to defend through demonstrable expertise, is so much easier to write than one which airs ideas.

In talks, presentations and the odd keynote address the focus is always much narrower and even though social media is inevitably involved there is little time or scope to get side-tracked and go down paths which ride the very edge of theory on social media and the web, like I have done here.

In including my ideas here I have tried to sketch for you, in as much detail as possible, the shape of things that are and the shape of things to come. To do so I have drawn on countless hours spent each day criss-crossing interdisciplinary facts and information and seeing in them, perhaps, trends and directions which few others do, at present.

Still, as my editor asked in a frustrated email after batting back and forth a dozen times the argument for the inclusion of a particular train of thought, 'Why take the risk?'.

Well, the rise of social media, as a web development tool is too great an opportunity not to talk about it at some length and not to share some of the things that keep me up late at night, trawling the web, thinking and testing when I should be asleep.

Take the practical stuff from here, as you should, but take also the concepts that go with it. Whether you are a student, a teacher, a businessman. A manager in a blue chip company or a guy with a startup and a handful of friends, think exactly where social media is taking us. Think about where you would want your business to be. Then work to make sure that what you achieve in a business sense works to further the conversation and create the kind of world you really want to do business in and we can all feel proud to be a part of.

Good luck.

David Amerland

# BIBLIOGRAPHY

Prodhan, Georgina (2011). *Survey: Marketers Struggle to Harness Social Media*, Reuters.
http://www.talkforumnyc.com/2011/10/11/survey-marketers-struggle-to-harness-social-media-reuters/

Macleod, Ishbel (2011). *Marketing chiefs overwhelmed by customer data on social media.*
http://www.thedrum.co.uk/news/2011/10/11/marketing-chiefs-overwhelmed-customer-data-social-media

Welsh, Jennifer (2011). *How search engines are messing with our minds.*
http://www.msnbc.msn.com/id/43759127/ns/technology_and_science-science

Lehreh, Jonah (2011). *How Friends Ruin Memory: The Social Conformity Effect,* Wired.
http://www.wired.com/wiredscience/2011/10/how-friends-ruin-memory-the-social-conformity-effect/

Carr, Nicholas (2011). *Is Google making us stupid?* The Atlantic.
http://www.theatlantic.com/magazine/archive/2008/07/is-google-making-us-stupid/6868/#

Report of Forrester Research's The State of Retailing Online 2011: Marketing, Social & Mobile,
http://www.shop.org/soro

Kahan, Dan M., Cultural Cognition as a Conception of the Cultural Theory of Risk (April 21, 2008). HANDBOOK OF RISK THEORY, S. Roeser, ed., Forthcoming; Harvard Law School Program on Risk Regulation Research Paper No. 08-20; Yale Law School, Public Law Working Paper No. 222. Available at SSRN: http://ssrn.com/abstract=1123807

Shipman, Tim, (2011). *Vince Cable: I sympathise with St Paul's protest... so we'll curb bosses' pay*, Daily Mail. http://www.dailymail.co.uk/news/article-2061003/Vince-Cable-I-sympathise-St-Pauls-protest--curb-bosses-pay.html

Kanai1,R. Bahrami, B. Roylance, R and Rees, G. (2011). *Online social network size is reflected in human brain structure*. Proceedings of the Royal Society B. http://rspb.royalsocietypublishing.org/content/early/2011/10/12/rspb.2011.1959.full

Dunbar R. I. M. (1998). *The social brain hypothesis. Evol. Anthropol. 6, 178–190.* (doi:10.1002/(SICI)1520-6505(1998)6:5<178::AID-EVAN5>3.0.CO;2-8) CrossRefWeb of Science.

Sparrow, B. Liu, J. Wegner, M. Daniel. (2011). *Google Effects on Memory: Cognitive Consequences of Having Information at Our Fingertips.* Science Mag. http://www.sciencemag.org/content/early/2011/07/13/science.1207745

Firas Khatib, Frank DiMaio, Foldit Contenders Group, Foldit Void Crushers Group, Seth Cooper, Maciej Kazmierczyk, Miroslaw Gilski, Szymon Krzywda, Helena Zabranska, Iva Pichova, James Thompson, Zoran Popović, Mariusz Jaskolski & David Baker. (2011) *Crystal structure of a monomeric retroviral protease solved by protein folding game players.* Nature Structural & Molecular Biology.
http://www.nature.com/nsmb/journal/v18/n10/full/nsmb.2119.html

Gray, Peter. (2011). *Why Children Protest Going to School: More Evolutionary Mismatch.* Psychology Today.
http://www.psychologytoday.com/blog/freedom-learn/201111/why-children-protest-going-school-more-evolutionary-mismatch

Purcell, Kristen. (2011). *Search and email still top the list of most popular online activities.* PEW Report.
http://www.pewinternet.org/~/media/Files/Reports/2011/PIP_Search-and-Email.pdf

# Acknowledgments

No author is an island. I am not sure if this was ever the case but in the information age this certainly is truer than ever. Similarly no book is ever the work of one person, exclusively. Authors may be the executive wing of the deal, we are the ones who get to do the hard work but each book has been shaped, added value to and contributed to in terms of ideas by all those who the author has talked to, corresponded with and burnt the midnight oil discussing things with. This book is no exception. The number of people who have been generous with their ideas, time and opinions is too numerous to mention here. The deal in publishing is that when it comes to a work of this magnitude someone has to be the public face of it and this usually falls to the author. The author also becomes the fall guy when thoughts, ideas and opinions, filtered through his mind cause reactions or create issues. Upon that note and in no certain order, thanks must go for their generosity and time when sharing ideas, to: Gregory Esau, Nora Eaves, Ted, Paul, Neil, Mark and the gang. Authors, by definition, need to be the reflective surfaces of society. While for many things in this world I am entirely blameless, when it comes to this work the blame is all mine.

Other Books by the same author

Lightning Source UK Ltd.
Milton Keynes UK
UKOW05f0629290317
297790UK00009B/125/P